RAISING
ARCHIE

The Story of Richard Morecroft and his Flying Fox

RAISING ARCHIE

The Story of Richard Morecroft and his Flying Fox

RICHARD MORECROFT

Photographs by Paul Sweeney and Michael Rayner

an ABC BOOK

SIMON & SCHUSTER
AUSTRALIA

RAISING ARCHIE

First published in Australasia in 1991 by
Simon & Schuster Australia
20 Barcoo Street, East Roseville NSW 2069

A Paramount Communications Company
Sydney New York London Toronto Tokyo Singapore

in association with the

Australian Broadcasting Corporation
150 William Street, Sydney NSW 2000

Text © 1991 Media Management Pty Ltd
Photographs © 1991 Simon and Schuster Australia

National Library of Australia
Cataloguing in Publication Data

Morecroft, Richard.
Raising Archie : the story of Richard Morecroft and
his flying fox.

ISBN 0 7318 0254 3.

1. Flying foxes. 2. Bats — New South Wales —
Ecology. I. Title.

599.409944

Designed by Jack Jagtenberg
Photography by Paul Sweeney and Michael Rayner
Cover photograph by Paul Sweeney
Typeset in Australia by Asset Typesetting Pty Limited
Produced by Mandarin Offset in Hong Kong

C O N T E N T S

FOREWORD

There is obviously a very big difference between saving a single member of a species of wild animal and the conservation of the world's nature as a whole, but the one can easily lead to the other. Just as it was vital to discover what Archie needed to keep him healthy and happy, it is just as important to learn how whole species interact with their habitats and with the other inhabitants.

Archie was lucky to have been so well looked after, but it would have been all for nothing had the rest of his species been facing extinction due to human intereference. Conservation means giving nature a healthy chance to co-exist with the human population and all its activities.

His Royal Highness The Duke of Edinburgh
International President of the World Wide
Fund for Nature

'd like to introduce you to a remarkable little animal. This is Archie. He's a baby flying fox whose mother died, so I'm looking after him for a while. Archie was only a few days old when he became an orphan. His mother was electrocuted on power lines, but when her body was removed from the wire, there was the baby still clinging to her. He was cold and thirsty, but he wasn't hurt.

Through the Wildlife Information and Rescue Service (known as WIRES) he was given food and kept warm until a volunteer foster parent could be found. And that was me. I'm a television newsreader for the Australian Broadcasting Corporation (ABC), but I'm also very interested in protecting and preserving wildlife, which is why I joined WIRES. WIRES is a voluntary organisation whose members look after orphaned or injured native animals so that eventually they can go back where they belong — into the wild. But it's important that the animals are looked after properly.

It's easy to make mistakes if you don't know what you're doing, so I'd recently taken a training course to learn how to care for various animals, including flying foxes. The course had been held in September because the breeding season for Grey Headed Flying Foxes gets underway around the end of that month. We were ready and waiting to look after the orphans that would be rescued and brought in for fostering. Archie was one of the first.

When Archie gets big enough and strong enough, he'll be able to go back into the wild and live a normal life with other flying foxes. But in the meantime, as a baby, he needs a lot of looking after. This is his story.

LIFE IN THE COLONIES

Flying foxes are large bats which are found along the eastern coast of Australia, and across many areas in the tropical north. There are a few different types of flying foxes — including Spectacled, Little Red, and Black — but the Grey Headed Flying Fox is the main variety found near Sydney in New South Wales.

Flying foxes usually live in big groups called colonies. Thousands of them live together, hanging from treetops during the day, sleeping, grooming themselves, and squabbling loudly about who's going to hang on which branch. (The more important you are as a flying fox, the higher up in the tree you get to hang.) If you look at a roosting colony, it seems as though the trees are covered with big black dangling fruits. These are the flying foxes at rest with their dark wings wrapped around their bodies.

Before white settlement of Australia, there were many hundreds of flying fox colonies scattered throughout the forests, but as those forests were cleared for farming and houses, the colonies were forced out or deliberately exterminated. Flying foxes were regarded simply as pests.

Now that there are cities and suburbs in places where once there was only bushland, there are not as many flying fox colonies any more.

Close to Sydney, for example, there's only one left. It's in a deep tree-filled valley surrounded by houses in one of the city's northern suburbs.

When flying fox mothers have small babies they carry them on their bodies all the time, whether they're hanging in the trees or flying at night. The young ones hold on tightly with their strong claws and mouth.

In the breeding season the mothers and babies form a group in the centre of the colony. And around the outer edge there are guards; their job is to keep an eye open for danger and to raise the alarm if anything frightens them.

Flying foxes don't usually feed in the trees where they roost during the day. Each evening as it starts to get dark, the whole colony takes to the air and flies off in many different directions to look for food. Then, before dawn, they all come back to the same place to spend the day together.

When the flying foxes head off at night around the city or its suburbs, there are often dangerous hazards along the way. Some flying foxes are electrocuted on power lines and occasionally they get caught on barbed-wire fences. A mother flying fox can sometimes die in one of these accidents, but the baby she is carrying may survive, hanging onto her body.

CHAPTER ONE

ARCHIE, I PRESUME?

I was at work in the ABC newsroom when I got the phone call. 'Can you pick up a baby flying fox tomorrow?' the WIRES office wanted to know. I said that, yes, I'd be delighted, but it wasn't until I put the phone down that I thought properly about the responsibility I'd just taken on. This was a little animal that was going to be completely dependent on me. For the next few months I was going to have to do everything for him that his mother would have done in the wild … except that I had to do it in my house or at work in a television station. It was exciting to think I'd be able to be so close to a wild animal as it grew up, but I was a bit nervous, too. What if it wouldn't eat properly? What if it got sick? And worst of all, what if, for some reason, it died?

That night when I got home from work I re-read all the notes I'd taken on the training course. Then the next morning I went to the local chemist and bought all the things necessary to sterilise a baby's feeding bottles. When I bought a little hairbrush as well, the chemist asked me if I had a new baby. I replied that I'd be picking one up in a few hours' time.

'Boy or girl?' the chemist asked.

'I'm not sure yet,' I answered, 'but it's quite furry and has small wings.'

The chemist looked at me strangely. It was the first of what would be many curious looks over the months to come, as people found out about my odd little orphan.

Five hours later I was sitting in my office at the ABC. It was mid-afternoon and on my desk in front of me, underneath the computer screen which glowed with the scripts of news stories and information from around the world, was a strange collection of objects: a large handkerchief, a plastic syringe, a box of tissues, a tiny hairbrush and a container of rather odd-smelling milk.

My little flying fox was hungry and I was going to have to feed

him by myself for the first time. I had to remember everything I'd been taught in the training classes and everything I'd seen done just a short time before in the living room of a Sydney suburban home.

It had been just before lunchtime when I'd arrived at the address I'd been given and knocked on the front door. The man who lived there, George, was a WIRES helper who'd been looking after the young flying fox for the few days since it had been found. I'd heard he'd raised quite a few orphaned animals, but it was still a surprise when he opened the door holding a large woollen sock with a baby possum's head peering out of it. I followed George into the living-room where he put away the possum. He then brought over a woven basket with a lid on it, which he put down gently on the table and opened. It was lined with soft cloths, and propped up against one side was what looked a bit like a large spring roll made out of a handkerchief. George lifted this little bundle out of the basket and at the bottom end of the rolled-up handkerchief I could see some dark fur. Carefully George passed it to me and, as I cradled it in my hands, the fur wriggled sleepily in the folds of the handkerchief. I could see two small soft ears, one of them wrinkled from being slept on. Then with another wriggle a tiny furry face slowly revealed itself. I couldn't help smiling when I saw that it was sucking contentedly on the last thing I would have expected to see in a wild animal's mouth — a small dummy. The tiny ears twitched as if each had a mind of its own and then, with a few sleepy blinks, two dark-brown sparkly eyes opened fully and looked up at me.

According to George, who'd measured and weighed it, the little flying fox was probably only about a week old. It was a young male. I asked about the dummy and George explained that in the wild, baby flying foxes hang on to one of their mother's nipples almost all the time, even when they're not actually taking milk, so a small rubber dummy gives them a sense of security.

'He's due to be changed and have a feed', said George. 'I thought you might like to have a go at doing it here so I can give you a few practical hints if you need them.' I said I thought that was a good idea. I had a feeling that a few practical hints would be very handy indeed.

'Well, first let's have a look at him. Have you seen one of these close-up before?' No, I replied, I hadn't. I was still enchanted by the deep liquid eyes that were peering up from above the tiny velvety nostrils. George started to unwrap the handkerchief. It was firmly folded all around the little flying fox because that way the baby feels well protected, as normally it would be wrapped up in its mother's wings. A few seconds later, as the handkerchief fell open, I had my first look at what it contained. There was a twisting, wriggling tangle of brown and gingery fur; thin, almost rubbery wings stretched over

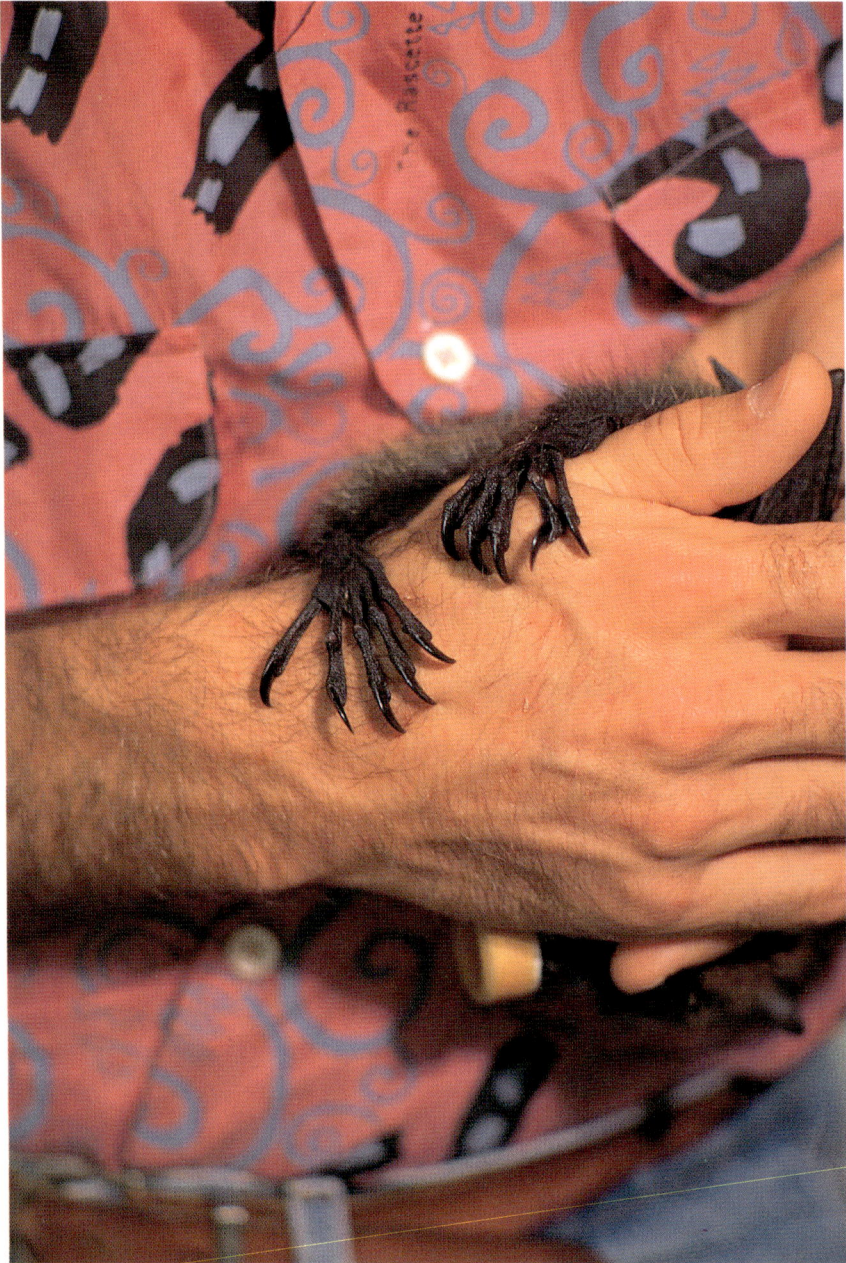

long fragile bones; and the most enormous monster-movie knobbly claws grabbing frantically at anything they could hang on to. This was my baby.

George skilfully removed a very messy piece of folded paper tissue from between the short legs, and wiped the fur.

'Certainly ready for that nappy change,' he said. 'Would you hold him while I get some clean tissues?'

The little flying fox had latched onto his fingers with its feet and was nestling comfortably into the palm of his hand. Its wings were folded neatly, but as I tried to persuade its clawed toes to move from George's fingers to mine, there was a scrabbling tangle of wings and talons. There seemed to be claws everywhere. On the front of each wing there was what looked like a short stick with a claw on it (it's actually the flying fox's thumb) and the clawed feet were like two bunches of hooks. I was amazed at how big they were compared to the rest of the flying fox's body, and how strong their grip was. They really were like something straight out of a horror film: black leathery skin with long, curved claws tipped with needle-sharp points.

As the little creature panicked slightly at my unfamiliar and unskilled handling, I felt its claws leaving tiny pinpricks all over my fingers. (I learned later that one trademark of a flying fox's foster parent is to have hands covered in scratches and small punctures. It's a tell-tale signature that can be recognised at a glance!)

Now I had the flying fox cradled in my hand. It was hanging upside-down, its feet hooked onto one of my fingers, and its head and body just slightly supported by my palm. The dummy moved a little from side to side and I just saw a tiny flash of deep pink tongue in the corner of its mouth. I don't know why, but the name Archie came into my head. It didn't seem to be a name that had any obvious connection with flying foxes. It seemed almost ridiculous as a name for an animal that within a year would be swooping through the night sky on powerful wings spanning a metre or so. But for this awkward little bundle of leathery skin, soft fur, oversized feet and wide brown eyes, it was exactly right. Archie. That would be his name.

I looked at him. He looked at me. One of the things I knew I had to get used to was upside-down eye contact. Like all bats, flying foxes

hang from their feet and they're most comfortable looking around at the world from that position. Archie and I were going to be spending a lot of time looking at each other like that over the months to come.

George was back with a box of tissues and a small stack of clean handkerchiefs. He'd also brought all the bits and pieces necessary to give Archie some special milk formula and he put them down on the table nearby.

'Now, you two,' said George, 'come over here and I'll guide you through a nappy change and a feed ...'

CHAPTER TWO

MILK AND NAPPIES

As I sat in my office, I thought back to what George had shown me and hoped I'd get it right by myself. The first challenge was to change Archie's nappy. It might sound a bit strange having to change a nappy for a baby animal — in fact it probably sounds pretty strange having a baby animal wearing a nappy in the first place — but for a young flying fox there are good reasons. In the wild its mother would keep its fur clean, but when it's being fostered by humans, that becomes our responsibility. As I mentioned before, the baby is wrapped up firmly in a large handkerchief so it feels the same security it would while being held in its mother's wings. However, without a small nappy of tissues and a regular change of handkerchiefs the little flying fox would quickly get very dirty fur. So regular nappy changes and fur cleaning are important. But for an L-plate foster parent they can also be quite a challenge — and my challenge was about to begin.

First, I laid out a clean handkerchief on the desk, folded it in half diagonally, and folded a tissue into a multi-layered strip.

Then Archie had to be unwrapped from his old hanky. His little

head poked out from one end and his dummy bobbed up and down as he watched me — I thought — with a slightly worried look in his eyes.

'I may not be all that good at this, Archie,' I said to him. 'You'll have to be patient with me. Just don't wriggle too much.' I unwrapped the handkerchief and as soon as Archie felt that he was no longer restrained, he wriggled. He wriggled a lot. He wriggled more than you would imagine it would be possible for an animal of his size to wriggle. His wings flapped about, but it was his feet that really showed a talent for movement. They grabbed at my fingers, got tangled in the handkerchief, got tangled in his old tissue nappy which immediately fell off (it wasn't too dirty I noticed with relief), got tangled with each other, got untangled from the handkerchief, got tangled with each other again, and eventually latched onto my hand with their sharp little claws in a way that said, 'Don't try to make me let go ...' His face peered over the edge of my fingers with alarm in his wide eyes, and his dummy bobbed up and down faster than before. We paused.

I managed to move him into a position where I could contain his wings and his body with one hand while cleaning the fur around his bottom with a warm damp tissue. As well as keeping his fur clean,

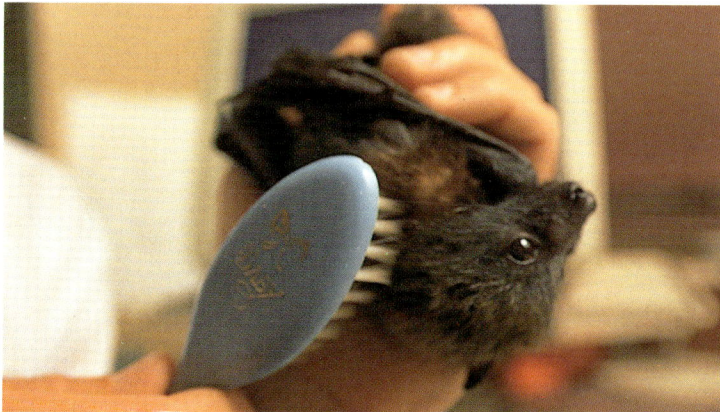

I knew it needed to be groomed carefully. Mothers spend a lot of time grooming their babies, so I picked up the soft brush I'd bought at

the chemist and started to stroke it gently through Archie's fur. He wriggled again at first, but then seemed to relax and enjoy it. Once he was well groomed, it was time to get him into a clean nappy and wrapped in a fresh handkerchief before I gave him a feed. This is how I did it:

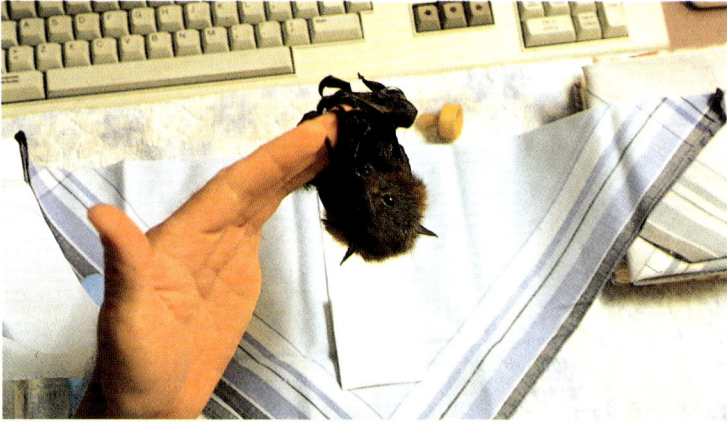

He was clinging to my fingers so the first job was to get him on his back with his head at the top of the handkerchief.

Then I had to get the new nappy of folded tissues between his legs. This involved a small tug of war because he was hanging on to my hand with his feet; but by lifting off one set of claws at a time I was able to get the nappy into position.

Next was the tricky part. One corner of the handkerchief had to be brought over and around his wings and body and tucked in behind him. But the hand which was holding him down was in the way. So I had to release him from my hand for a moment, get the hanky into place and then let his feet come up and grab the handkerchief instead of my hand.

Then the bottom corner of the hanky came up over his feet …

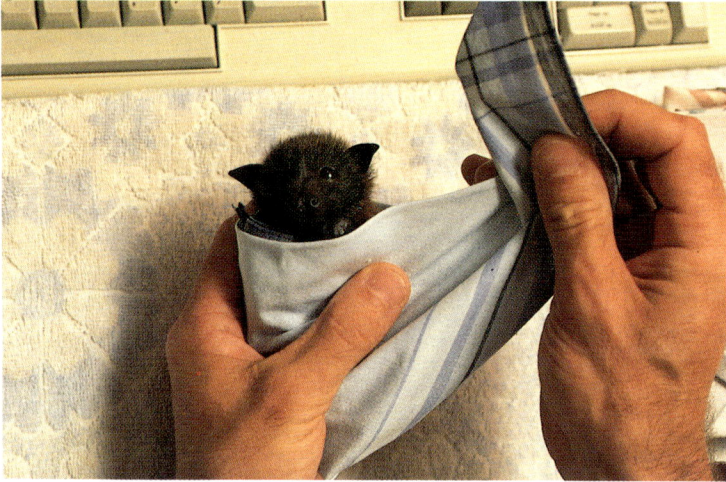

... and finally the remaining part of the handkerchief had to be brought over the top and around the whole package so that Archie was securely wrapped.

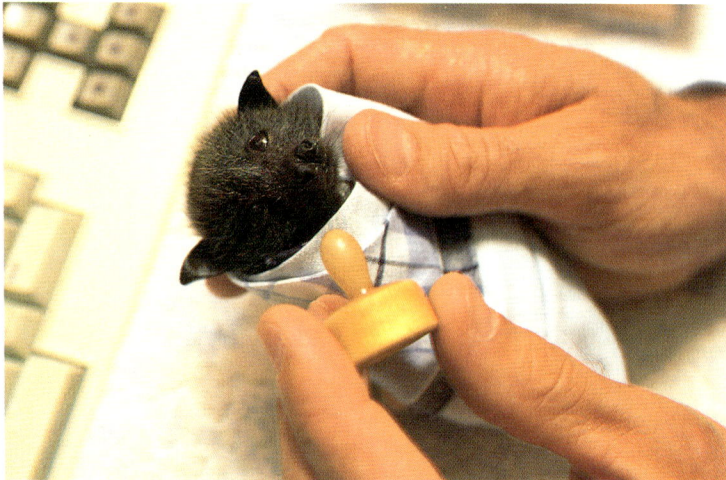

Success! Now that he was once again looking like a fat spring roll with a furry head poking out of one end, it was time for Archie to be fed.

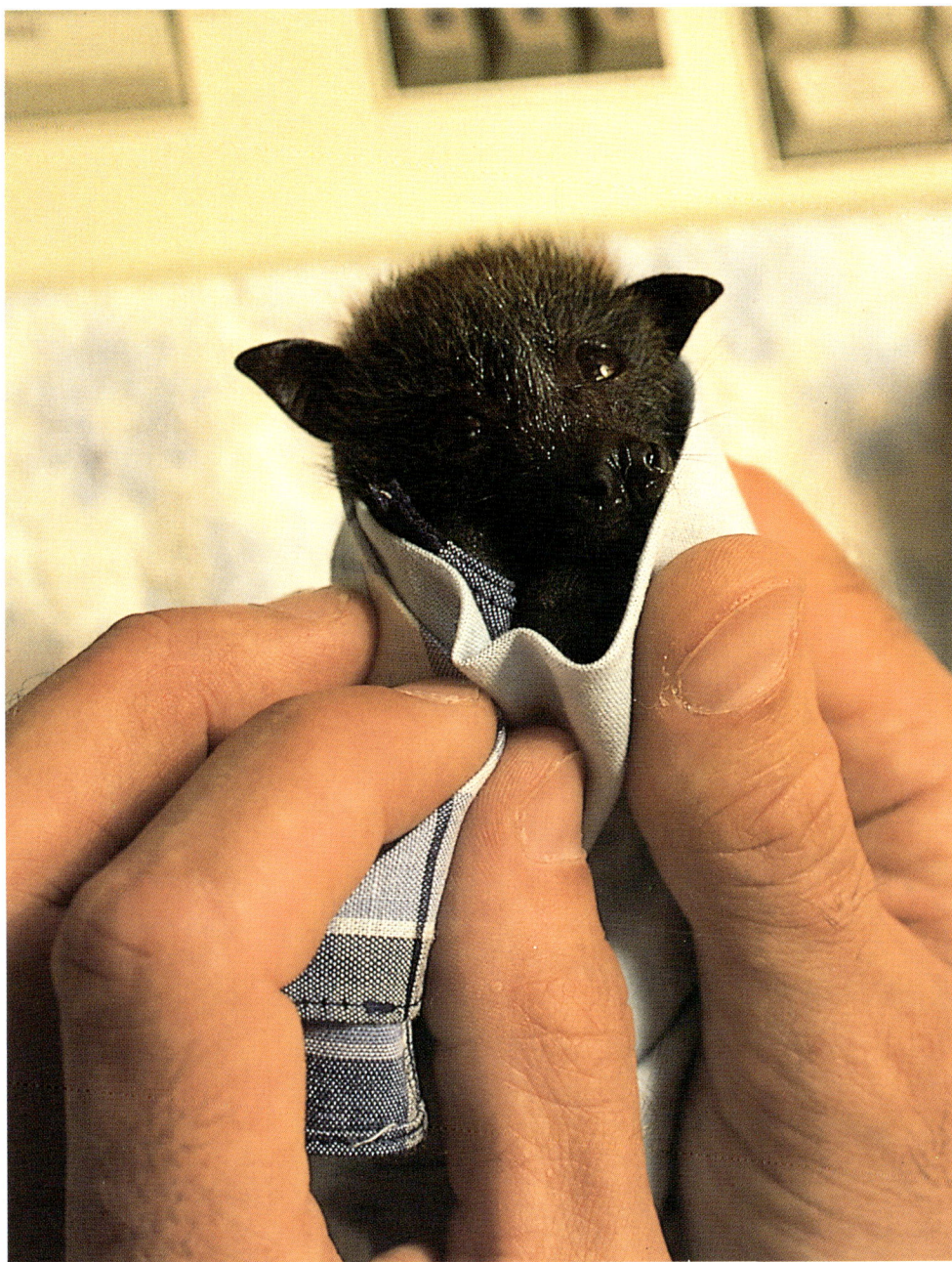

I had made up some special milk formula (yes, amazingly, you can buy a powdered formula specially for baby flying foxes … and others for wombats, kangaroos, and possums as well!) and I'd brought it to work with me in a little jar. It had been warming in a bowl of hot water while I was changing Archie, so now I put him down and picked up the syringe I had nearby. I carefully sucked the right amount of milk up into it and then put the rubber teat over the end. The teat is designed to be the same shape in the baby's mouth as its mother's nipple so that it won't feel too strange to a young flying fox. I made sure there were no air bubbles trapped in the syringe or the teat and then squeezed a couple of drops of milk onto the inside of my wrist. This was to check that the formula was warm enough, but not too hot. It was just right.

Archie's nostrils were quivering, and his ears moved back and forth

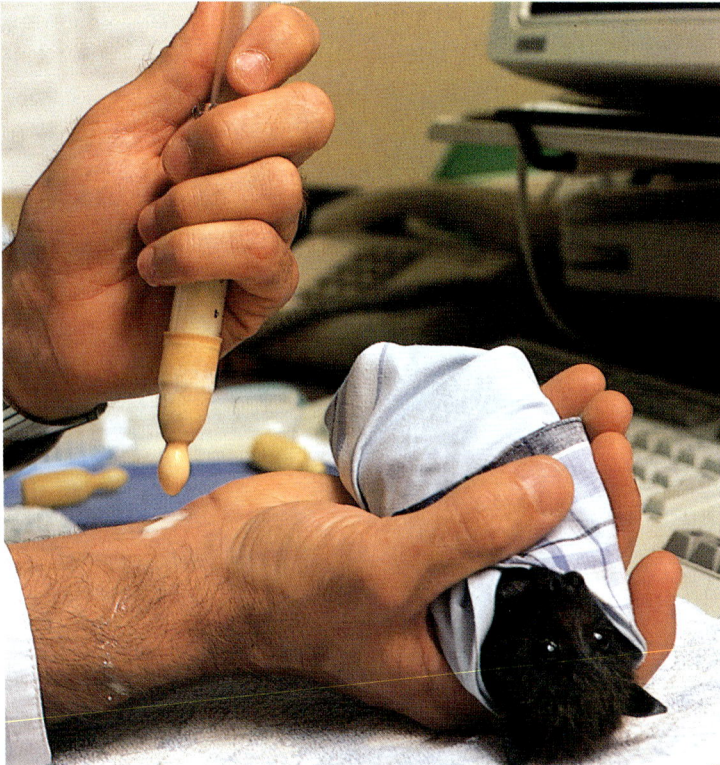

quite independently of each other — a sure sign of interest. I picked him up in his wrapping and held him sloping downwards. Most baby animals (not to mention baby humans) would choke if you tried to make them feed with their head lower than their body, but for a flying fox, of course, it's the other way round. We'd been warned in our training class that flying foxes are used to eating upside down and that a baby would have problems if we didn't keep its head nice and low while we were feeding it.

Archie could smell the milk, and without any prompting, dropped his dummy onto the desk and stretched out towards the syringe. I moved it closer and touched the teat against his lips. He hesitated for just a moment, then opened his mouth, grabbed the teat, and started sucking for all he was worth.

This was very lucky because I knew that sometimes baby flying

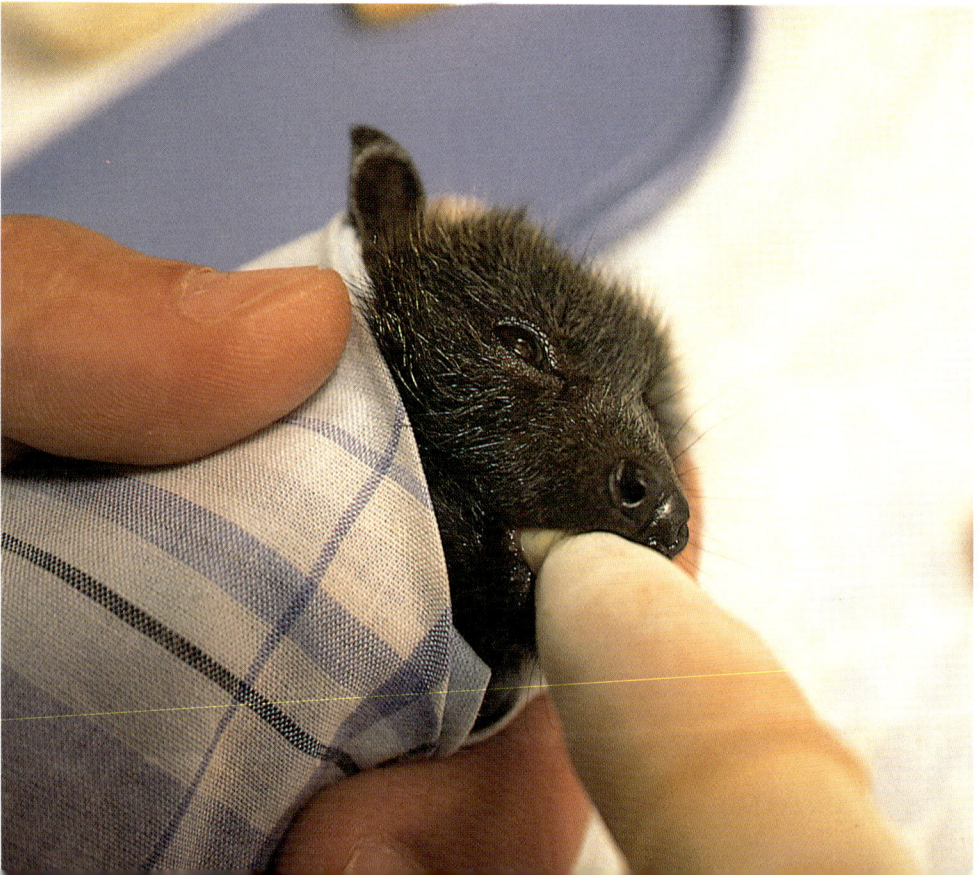

foxes take a while to accept a rubber teat as an alternative to their mother. They either refuse to open their mouth, or they bite the teat, or they just hold it in their mouth without actually sucking on it. In the few days George had been looking after him, Archie must have got used to the idea of rubber providing milk, because he was sucking very happily now. It didn't take more than a few minutes before he'd finished the formula in the syringe and was just sucking hopefully on the empty teat. He peered up at me as if to say, 'More?', and for a moment I wondered whether I should have called him Oliver instead of Archie. But I knew it was important that he only have a certain amount of milk because the formula had been carefully planned so that a young flying fox would grow at the right rate. Too much wouldn't be good for him, but it wasn't easy to persuade him of that. He didn't want to let go of the teat even though the flow of milk had stopped. He hung on grimly, as he would have done in the wild while his mother moved about in the trees. (It wouldn't be long before I'd discover just how determinedly a young flying fox can lock its jaws onto something — but that's a story for later.)

Anyway, there was a bit of pulling and persuading before finally Archie let go of the teat and I offered him his dummy instead. He grabbed that and then looked around him, his ears twitching, alert for every sound, his round brown eyes sparkling. I found myself smiling and thinking what a beautiful little animal he was. I hoped that by raising him through these vulnerable months until he was strong and independent enough to be released I could help give him the life in the wild he deserved. I was looking forward to the time we would be spending together when I could watch him grow and develop. And now we'd passed the hurdle of the first solo nappy change and feed, I felt a bit more confident. I had really started the job of raising Archie ...

looked at my watch and realised I was due down in the television studio to record a segment of script for the news that night. I left my office in rather a mess, but decided I'd have to clean up the syringe and the other bits and pieces after I'd done the recording. I just hoped that no-one would poke their head around the office door while I was away; a baby's hairbrush, an empty syringe and several rather messy tissues all sitting on my desk would provide, well … at least a mystery.

I took Archie with me down to the studio because there was one important part of caring for him that meant we needed to stay close. Archie had to be kept warm. Very young flying foxes can't control their own body heat for a few weeks after they're born, so they need to be kept at a temperature which is just right for them; not too hot, and not too cold. In the wild they're close to their mother's skin all the time and often wrapped in the warmth of her wings. One way of giving Archie that warmth was to keep him close to my skin, so that's what I did.

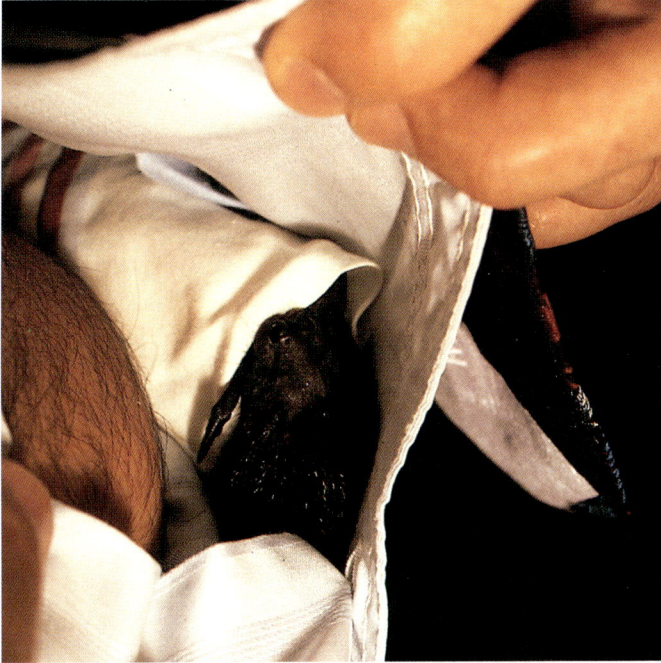

I unbuttoned the lower part of my shirt and carefully slipped the well-wrapped Archie inside. He lay quite comfortably on the natural shelf formed where my shirt tucked into my trousers.

I re-buttoned the shirt, slipped on my jacket and went to sit down behind the news desk.

The Archie bundle made quite a bulge in my shirt, but with a little bit of adjustment and by bringing my jacket carefully around to close over the top of the bump, it looked all right.

No-one would be able to tell that underneath the suit, shirt and tie there were two hearts beating; one belonging to a small furry animal wrapped in a handkerchief and sucking a dummy …

And that was how I read the news for many evenings afterwards. Thousands of viewers were unaware that each night a baby flying fox was a part of their news service, and Archie heard more information about international events and political intrigues than any flying fox had ever done before. There were some nights, though, that Archie spent the news half-hour being looked after by various other people in the newsroom. There was much curiosity about this strange little baby I'd acquired, and one or two people were particularly happy to take care of him for a little while. So Archie was kept warm inside a variety of shirts, blouses and jumpers.

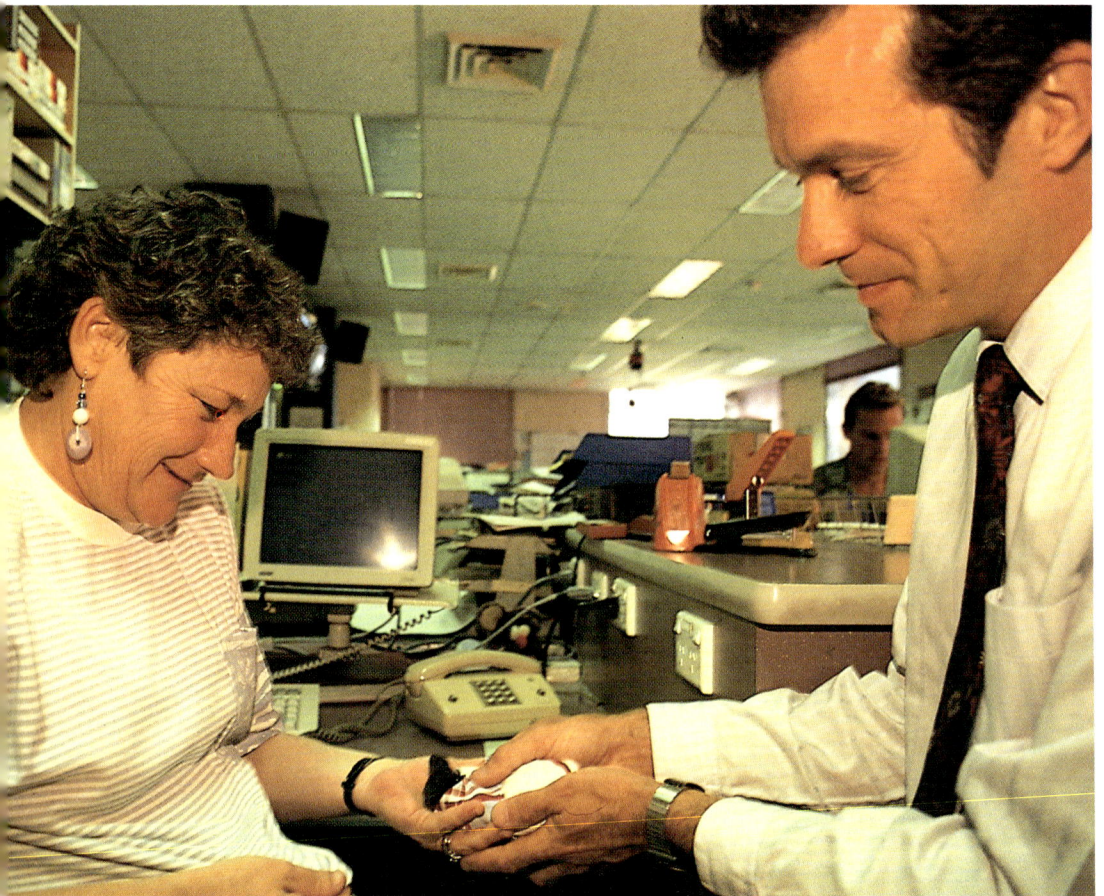

Most of the time during the days and evenings that Archie was carried around inside my shirt he was no problem at all. He made a bit of a bulge, but wrapped up in his handkerchief he lay there quite happily. However, one night was a little different. It was a particularly warm evening and I was having dinner with some friends in a restaurant. As usual, Archie was inside my shirt and before we arrived at the restaurant everyone in our party had wanted to have a look at him. Archie had been a model of charm and good behaviour. Soon after we sat down, though, he started to get a bit restless. Perhaps the warmth of the evening made him uncomfortable or perhaps I just hadn't wrapped him up very well, but one way or another he was restless and he wriggled. He wriggled until I realised that he'd managed to get out of his handkerchief. It wasn't hard to tell, because all his sharp little claws were scrabbling around against the skin of my stomach and ribs. And he was on the move, too. I could feel him crawling along the bottom of my shirt towards my back. I put my hand over him outside the shirt and tried to hold him still but he wriggled even more and his claws scratched and tickled so much I didn't know whether to laugh or say ouch.

'What's wrong?' asked one of my friends.

'Archie's escaped from his hanky and has gone exploring inside my shirt,' I said. 'I'll have to go to the toilet so I can get him out and re-wrap him.'

Unfortunately the toilets were right on the other side of the room from where we were sitting, which meant walking the full distance of the crowded restaurant trying to hold Archie still. Quite a number of people looked at me oddly as I navigated my way between the tables, and it's hard to imagine what they thought was going on. My friends, of course, knew what was inside my shirt, but the other diners in the restaurant didn't. What they saw was a man walking slowly and purposefully towards the toilets, carefully clutching a bulge on one side of his stomach which every now and then could be seen to move slightly under his hand. And when it moved, he seemed either to wince or suppress laughter. A number of people actually stopped eating as I edged past them, and one woman looked quite worried as Archie

PESTS AND POLLINATORS

For more than a century, flying foxes have been thought of mainly as agricultural pests. When bushland has been cleared and orchards planted, flying foxes have often raided the fruit trees. Over the years, forest clearing and fruitgrowers have wiped out hundreds of thousands of flying foxes, drastically reducing the number of colonies since white settlement.

There's no doubt that flying foxes can badly damage a fruit crop, but research shows that, given the choice, flying foxes prefer to eat their natural foods — eucalyptus blossoms, rainforest fruits, wild figs, and even some types of tree bark — rather than introduced fruits like apples, apricots and peaches. The trouble is that so much bushland has been cleared that natural fruits and blossoms are often in short supply, so the flying foxes have to look for alternatives.

We should remember, however, that flying foxes have an important role to play in helping the growth of forests. Through feeding on blossoms in the wild they carry pollen from flower to flower, and the seeds from the native fruits they eat are spat out or scattered in their droppings, which encourages the spread of new trees.

gave an especially large twitch as I squeezed by her table.

Once I arrived in the washroom I undid my shirt and managed to grab Archie and drag him out. I was just re-wrapping him in his handkerchief when another diner walked in from the restaurant. He couldn't help but see me — or, more to the point, Archie — and he asked, 'What have you got there?' I showed him and explained how I was fostering Archie. The man said, 'A flying fox? We used to call them fruit bats. My uncle had an orchard and I remember when I was a teenager he'd take us out shooting them at weekends. I thought they were just a pest.' I told him they were protected these days, and we talked for a few minutes about what flying foxes like to eat and why they could be a problem for fruit growers.

I got a few more strange looks as I walked back to my table, only this time I didn't have to cover Archie with my hand. The bulge on one side of my stomach was still there, but at least it wasn't moving. As I sat down I could see the man I'd met talking to the other people at his table. Some of them were shaking their heads and others were glancing over towards our table with worried looks on their faces. I smiled at them and gently patted the lump in my shirt. But it was a reminder for me that flying foxes have not traditionally been very popular animals.

CHAPTER THREE

BEDTIME AND BATHTIME

Over the next few days I began to get into the routine of raising Archie. In many ways it was like looking after a human baby — the regular feeds, the changing of nappies, and the careful washing and sterilisation of feeding equipment. Archie had four feeds a day; first thing in the morning, then at lunchtime, dinnertime and last thing at night before I went to sleep.

That final feed usually took place in my bed. I'd warm the milk and have all the clean handkerchiefs and tissues ready on the bedside table. Then, propped up with pillows, I'd sit and cradle Archie in my hands while he guzzled away. It was always very important not to let too much milk into his mouth at once because of the danger of it being inhaled. That can result in lung infection and is one of the most common causes of death amongst young flying foxes being fostered. I always worried about it, so feeding was a slow, careful process with a slightly impatient Archie sucking hard as if to say, 'Come on, come on, I can take more than that — give me a decent mouthful!'

The other thing I used to worry about was this. Every night after I'd finished feeding and wrapping Archie I'd put him into his specially heated cage. And every night I'd go back to bed, go to sleep and dream that I'd dozed off while feeding him. In this dream I'd rolled over and squashed Archie underneath me. I'd find myself waking up, carefully trying to lift my body away from the mattress and feeling around on the sheet for a little flattened flying fox, before I woke properly and realised that, once again, it was just a dream. I had this nightmare as reliably as clockwork every night that I fed Archie in bed. I tried to beat it by reminding myself as I closed my eyes that Archie was safely in his cage, but still it kept coming back. I resigned myself to being a hopelessly neurotic parent.

The cage I mentioned was one of the animal transport variety with a plastic bottom and wire top. It was rather sturdier than Archie really needed at the time, as he wasn't exactly a Houdini in his handkerchief. In fact a basket with a secure lid would have done just as well. But I happened to have the cage available and I knew it would come in handy as Archie grew a bit. At night the cage was put on top of a special electric heating pad which gently maintained a constant warmth. This fulfilled the same function as my body when I carried Archie around in my shirt during the day. There was no problem while there was a ready source of electricity for the heating pad, but the second weekend I had Archie I'd arranged to go camping in the bush and there were certainly no power points handy out there.

While I was awake it was fine because Archie could stay in my shirt. But I'd decided that night-time warmth would have to be supplied by a well-wrapped hot-water bottle in his cage. It was important to have the hot-water bottle good and hot so it would last for as long as possible, but that meant it had to be heavily wrapped in towels so it didn't give out heat too quickly and raise the temperature to a level dangerous for Archie.

As night fell and I started to prepare for bed, I put the billy on the camp stove to warm up some water. A few minutes later I had an interesting challenge trying to pour a steaming stream from the billy into the narrow neck of the hot-water bottle. (You try it sometime … perhaps I just need more practice with a billy.) Anyway, eventually the 'hottie' was filled, thoroughly wrapped up, and put on the bottom of Archie's cage. I had brought a thermometer which I put amongst the folds of the blanket that would soon hold Archie in his handkerchief. That complete package would then sit on top of the towel-clad hottie. After a couple of minutes I checked the thermometer and realised to my horror that if I'd put Archie in there straight away, he'd probably have cooked! (I know that roast flying fox is considered a delicacy in some cultures, but I certainly didn't want Archie on my menu.) So I added another two layers of towelling around the hot water bottle, and waited several minutes until the thermometer had stabilised at the right level. Then I tucked Archie in and brought the cage into the tent with me. I

FLYING FOX FACTS

(For the Grey Headed Flying Fox)

WINGSPAN:
Over 1 metre
HEAD AND BODY LENGTH:
About 25 centimetres
WEIGHT:
About 700 grams
LIFESPAN:
Up to 15 years
MATING SEASON:
March to April
BREEDING SEASON:
October (only one baby is born to each female)
NORMAL FLIGHT RANGE:
Up to 30 or 40 kilometres per night

PARASITES:
No fleas or lice
SMELL:
Distinctive odour from glands near their shoulders
NUMBER OF COMMUNICATION SOUNDS:
More than 20
NATURAL FOODS:
Eucalypt blossoms, nectar, berries, figs, rainforest fruits, occasional tree bark
NUMBER OF INDIVIDUALS IN A COLONY:
From several hundred to thirty or forty thousand

tucked myself in, zipped up my sleeping bag and closed my eyes.

A moment later they were wide open again. I had forgotten something vital. I rummaged in my rucksack and pulled out the little alarm clock I'd brought along. As anyone who's gone to bed with a hot hot-water bottle will tell you, they don't stay that way all night. By the time you wake up in the morning, it feels as though there's a large cold slug next to your feet. I would have to keep refilling Archie's hottie so his temperature didn't drop too much. But how quickly does a hottie become a coldie? I didn't know. I hadn't done this before. I took a deep breath and set the alarm for two hours later.

I lay back in my sleeping bag. I looked at the roof of the tent. I listened to the frogs and the crickets. Somewhere nearby I heard the thump of a wallaby in the scrub. I tried to go to sleep. Was Archie really warm enough, I wondered. Perhaps now he'd been in there for a while I should check again. I wriggled free of the top of my sleeping bag, fumbled around for the torch, clicked it on and dug around for the thermometer in Archie's blanket. Mmmmmm, it felt nice and warm in there.

'Warmer than my sleeping-bag on this chilly night,' I thought with a little shiver. The thermometer was still registering a good, even temperature so I tucked it back in. Wriggling down into the sleeping-bag again I thought, 'I hope I hear the alarm go off.' I closed my eyes.

I woke with a start, wondering for a second or two where I was and then remembering. 'I've missed the alarm!' I thought. I fumbled to find the clock in the darkness and when I did I peered at its face. It was only half an hour later. I sighed and lay back again. The frogs and crickets continued to sing. I drifted into sleep.

The jangling alarm made my heart beat wildly. My arms were caught in the sleeping-bag and I couldn't find the zipper. Eventually I did, and let myself out to silence the clock. When I inspected the hot-water bottle I found it had cooled, but only a little.

'Still,' I thought, 'I'd better refill it and then I can leave it next time for three hours instead of two.' Pulling on a jumper, I crawled out of the tent into the cold night air and heated some more water on the stove. Still splashing a lot onto the ground, I refilled the hot-water bottle and wrapped it up again. Archie and his thermometer were carefully put back in the cage and my body was carefully put back in the sleeping-bag.

I think I woke up at least twice in the next three hours thinking that I'd missed the alarm. Eventually it did ring and I stumbled bleary-eyed through the refilling procedure again. This was not a relaxing way to spend a night, I decided. If Archie could have said anything, I think he would have agreed. As I lifted him in and out of his cage to change the hottie he tried to pull his head as far as he could down into his handkerchief wrapping, rather like someone pulling the blankets up around their ears to block out a noise. That night, as far as Archie was concerned, I was a nuisance. But at least he stayed warm …

Another procedure Archie didn't approve of — a serious disturbance — was bathtime. As I've mentioned, mother flying foxes keep their babies very clean; but with the best will in the world, damp tissues and cotton buds just can't do the same job. Sometimes more thorough washing is called for to loosen obstinate pieces of caked-on dirt and to flush underarms (or underwings, if you prefer) and tricky folds of skin. That special cleaning reduces the risk of fungal infection — and, as you can imagine, it would be no fun for a small bat to get a bad case of athlete's wing …

Anyway, how do you give a baby flying fox a bath? Well you put it under the tap, of course! Seriously, that's what you do. The temperature of the water flowing from the tap has to be carefully fixed so it's just warm, but not at all hot. And the flow mustn't be strong enough to cause any splashing. Then it's a case of holding the body and one wing firmly in one hand and stretching out the other wing with the other hand so water can flow over the fur and the wing membrane. With a little bit of gentle finger rubbing, any dirt is massaged away. Then the process is repeated for the other wing.

Sounds simple. But add a wildly wriggling, flapping little flying fox who's never been in a sink underneath a tap before, and has decided that it's high on the list of things he doesn't want to do in life. It's not so easy then …

Mind you, the first time I tried to bath Archie, I made a big mistake. Without really thinking, I took his dummy out of his mouth as I was doing the final temperature check of the water. After all, you wouldn't have a dummy in the bath, would you? Perhaps if I'd actually been able to ask Archie that question, he'd have given me a straight answer and saved me a lot of trouble. As it was, he looked distinctly unsettled as I put his dummy down on the edge of the basin.

I should mention that this bath took place soon after I'd arrived home one night after doing the news. I was going out to a special dinner so I'd changed into a formal shirt and bow-tie, but I decided I had enough time to give Archie a quick bath before I went out. As it turned out, it was not good planning at all.

As soon as I got Archie under the stream of water he wriggled

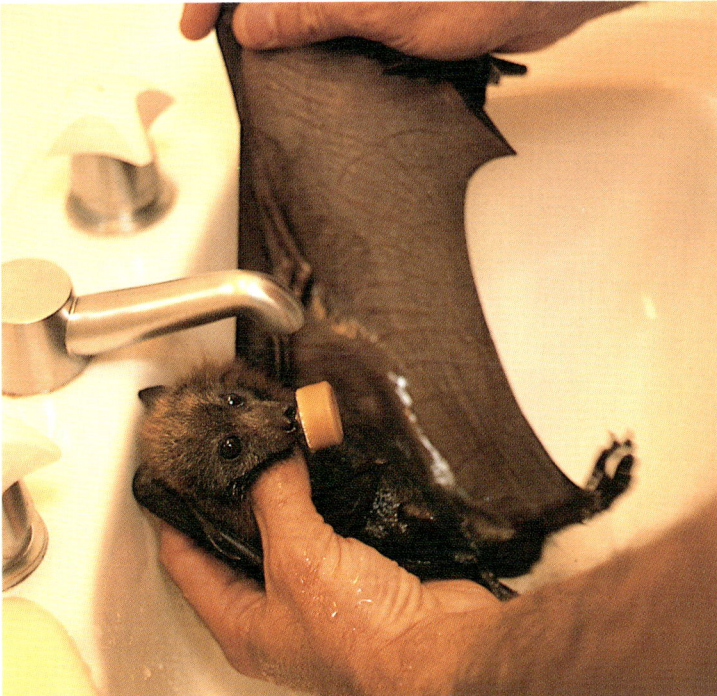

furiously, his feet grabbing at my hands and his wings flicking spray everywhere. We battled for a few minutes, but eventually I was able to rub his fur and that all-important area where his wings join his body. A quick rinse and he was done.

'There, that wasn't too bad was it?' I asked him. His eyes looked back at me in a way which said quite clearly, 'Yes it was ...' He was still wriggling damply, his bedraggled fur a wet tangle on his little round stomach. I suddenly realised that I hadn't brought a small towel in for him.

'Oh well,' I thought, 'I'll just have to use one of the bathtowels here.' It was important that he was dried thoroughly so he didn't get a chill.

So, holding him carefully, I took a towel off the rail and wrapped it around him. He seemed to calm down a lot once he was enclosed in the towel, and when I opened the folds to start drying his fur I saw why. I also saw why it would have been a good idea to leave his dummy in his mouth. He had grabbed a small fold of towelling between his teeth and was sucking on it with great determination. I tried to pull it out of his mouth, but he clamped his jaws together and looked sideways at me. The message was clear. He was going to hang on.

I assumed he would let go after a minute or so when he calmed down, so I simply had to dry him while he chewed grimly on the towel. Trying to dry a small flying fox with a large bathtowel — especially when one end of the flying fox is firmly attached to that bathtowel — is quite a challenge. And when all of the many available claws get caught in each little towelling loop it makes it even more interesting. Anyone watching me at a distance may not have noticed Archie and might simply have assumed I was wrestling with some complicated type of bathtowel origami.

Archie was eventually dry, but his jaws were still locked tightly on the towel. And I was due to go out to that dinner — overdue in fact. The problem was that it was a very big bathtowel. It couldn't go in Archie's cage with him because he'd get squashed if I tried to force it into that space, and I certainly couldn't wrap him up in it and tuck the huge bundle inside my shirt. I held Archie (and the towel) up close to my face. I looked at him. He looked at me.

'Archie,' I said, 'I have to go out, and I have to go out now.' He tucked his chin tightly into his chest and looked sideways at me again, a little crescent of white showing on one side of his deep brown iris. In my imagination a small voice said, 'Tough ...'

'If you don't let go, Archie, I'm going to be very late.' I was using my firmest voice, but in flying fox language it meant nothing. I wondered if there was a flying fox noise that meant 'Let go'. I'd heard that flying foxes have more than twenty different voice signals and communicate a lot in their colonies, but that wasn't much help. I tried again to wiggle the towel out of his mouth, but his jaw muscles tightened and I was afraid of damaging his teeth if I pulled too hard.

'Come on, Archie, this is very silly. Please ...' I couldn't help but smile. It *was* very silly. A TV newsreader in full dinner dress was pleading with a small furry animal to stop biting his bathtowel. And the small furry animal was saying no.

'Archie, it can't be any fun having a mouthful of towelling. You'll enjoy your dummy much more ...'

'Of course,' I thought suddenly. 'Who's being the dummy here?' I put Archie down carefully on the bed in the towel and went into the bathroom to get his dummy. If I rubbed it gently against the side of his mouth then perhaps he'd let go of the towel and grab hold of the dummy instead. I came back into the bedroom, secret weapon in hand, and there was Archie, cheerfully climbing up the pillow having left the towel behind him. I grabbed him, holding his wings against his body with one hand, and popped the dummy into his mouth. He sucked on it with great enthusiasm and I heard that small voice in my imagination say, 'Well, it's about time you gave me that. I was heading off to find it myself.'

'And next time,' I thought, 'I'll make sure I leave your dummy in for every drop and splash of bathtime.'

I quickly wrapped him up with a clean nappy and handkerchief and put him in his cage with the heater on. I raced out to the car, and yes, I was late for the dinner; but when I explained to people that I'd had a young flying fox stuck on my bathtowel they understood the problem. Well, I think they did.

CHAPTER FOUR

JOINING WEIGHTWATCHERS

Explaining to people about Archie did sometimes pose a challenge; I think, as much as anything else, because they just weren't expecting a baby flying fox to be a part of their life on that particular day. A good example was the first time I took Archie to the post office. I wasn't trying to get rid of him, it was simply the best place to get him weighed.

One of the most important aspects of looking after a young flying fox is to make sure that it's growing at the right rate. You can do that partly by measuring the length of its body and its forearm bones, but more importantly by keeping track of its weight increase. Because it's a fairly small animal, even if it's growing well it will only add small amounts of weight; and that means increases need to be measured carefully and accurately. Some really top quality kitchen scales might do the trick, but I didn't even have any basic ones, so I went for the other option — the post office. The scales there for weighing airmail letters and small parcels are very accurate … and they're ideally suited to weighing small wrapped-up flying foxes as well.

So that's why I took my small wrapped-up flying fox to a post office. His first weighing session unfortunately wasn't at my regular post office, although perhaps given the confusion and mixed messages of that first trip it was just as well. I called in at a post office on my way to the ABC and joined the short queue at the counter. Archie was wrapped up inside my shirt under my jacket, so was well hidden. When it was my turn, the woman behind the counter beckoned me forward.

'Yes,' she said, still looking down at some letters she was sorting, 'what would you like?' As she looked up, I reached inside my shirt and pulled out the bundle containing Archie. I saw her eyes register some alarm even before the package was revealed. I suppose not too many people reach inside their shirts to pull out their letters. Perhaps she thought I was a robber about to threaten her with a hidden weapon. Anyway, she looked relieved when she saw the handkerchief, but then uncertain as I said, 'I'd like to weigh this please.'

'What is it?' she asked, stepping back just a little from the counter.

Now I should point out that over the preceding few days since I had first acquired Archie, I'd become quite used to people being fascinated by him, finding him loveable and appealing, and being enthusiastically curious about him. I mention this because it explains a little why rather than cautiously saying, 'This is a young native animal that I'm looking after. It's called a flying fox and I need to keep a careful check on its weight', I actually answered her 'What is it?' question by simply saying, 'Here, have a look.' She leant hesitantly towards me, and I pulled back the handkerchief a little so she could clearly see Archie's face. Usually the sight of his sparkly brown eyes and mobile ears would provoke smiles and comments of 'Isn't he sweet' but in this case there was a different response. She screamed. Not loudly, in a dramatic Hollywood way (it was more like a little yelp of alarm really) but clearly enough for everyone else in the post office to turn towards us and wonder what was going on.

'I'm sorry. I didn't mean to frighten you,' I said. 'It's just a little flying fox.'

'A little what?' she asked.

'A flying fox. It's, er … it's a type of bat. You know, with wings.'

'A bat?'

'Yes. I'm looking after it and I need to weigh it accurately to check that I'm feeding it the right amount.'

'Well, won't it fly around?'

'No, it's only very young. It'll stay wrapped up in this handkerchief.'

'And you want to put it on the scales?'

'Yes please.' She thought for a second and then said, 'I'll have to speak to the manager.' She ducked out through a swinging door to the back part of the post office and was gone for a few moments. During this time a couple of the other customers were quite interested in having a look at Archie and I began to explain to them what I was doing. But I hadn't got far when the manager came out.

'Excuse me, sir,' he said. I broke off my mini-lecture with the other customers.

'Oh, sorry … yes, hello.'

'Excuse me, but I understand that you want to weigh a rat,' he said.

'What? Oh no, no,' I said, 'a flying fox.'

'I was told that you had a rat in a handkerchief and you wanted to weigh it.'

'No, I haven't got a rat, I've got a bat—a flying fox actually—and yes, I would like to weigh it please.'

'On our scales?'

'Yes, please.'

'You don't want to send it anywhere do you?'

'No, I don't …'

'Because it's prohibited to send animals through the post.'

'No, no, I definitely don't want to send it anywhere. I'd just like to weigh it accurately so I can keep track of its weight gain.'

'Oh, I see,' he said, although I'm not sure that he did. 'Well I don't suppose that should be too much of a problem, should it? Not really. But, er … could I have a look at it?' I showed him Archie's head poking out of the handkerchief.

'Hmmm … It um … it does look a bit like a rat,' he said doubtfully.

'Well, believe me, it's not,' I said, in what I hoped was my most believable voice. 'It's a young flying fox and it has wings.'

'Wings?' he asked. 'It won't … ?'

'No, it won't fly around. It'll stay wrapped up like this.'

'Ah. Right. Well I suppose you'd better weigh it then.'

And so I did.

Over the next few weeks I went through Archie's weighing procedure many times, usually at my local post office where they seemed to take it all rather more in their stride. In fact they became quite interested in Archie's progress and would take the little bundle from me and put Archie on the scales themselves.

It wasn't just a case of weighing Archie wrapped up in his handkerchief. To get a precise weight for Archie himself I would first

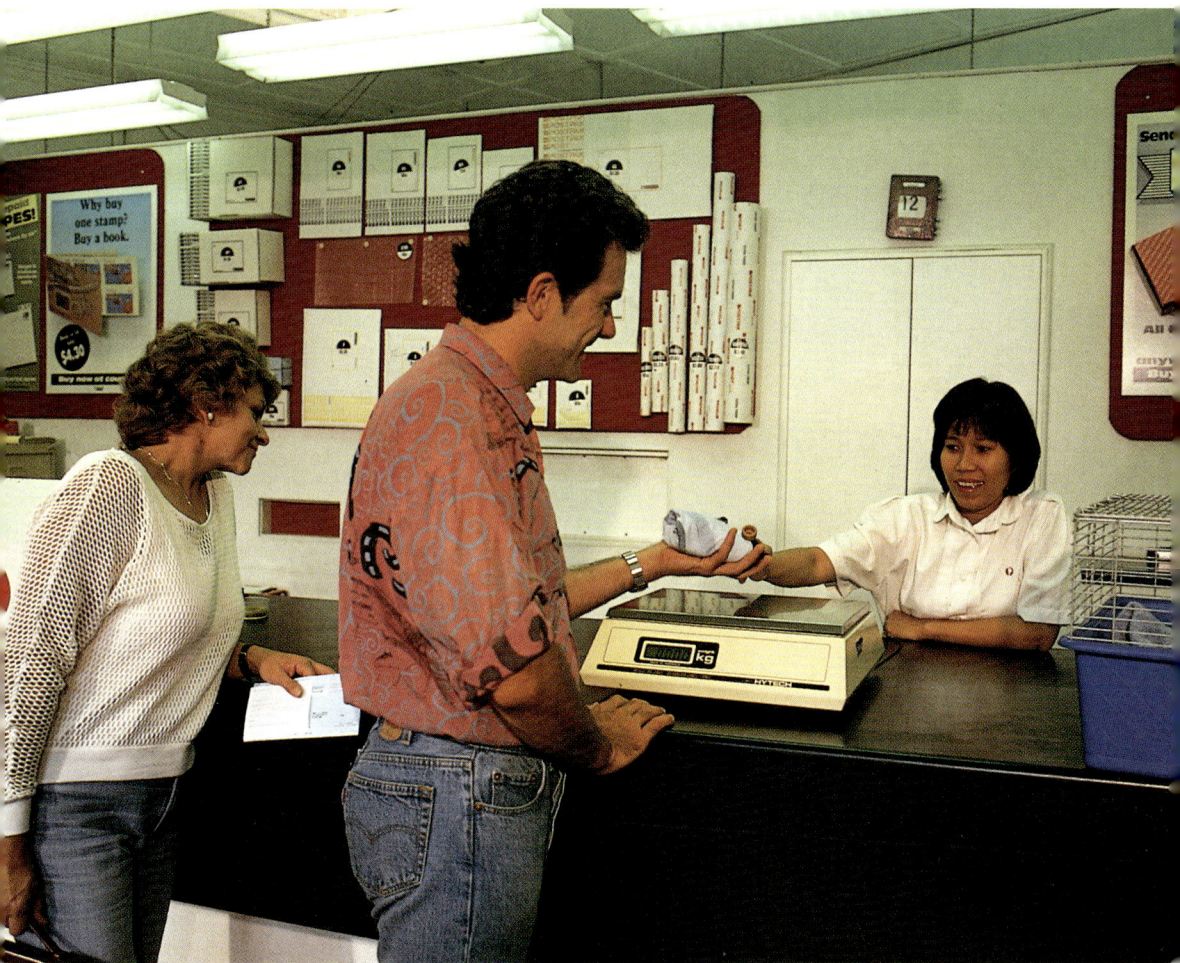

weigh a handkerchief the same size as the one he was in. And tucked into that hanky were folded tissues the same as his nappy, and a spare dummy.

Then when Archie went on the scales complete with handkerchief, nappy and dummy of his own, I could subtract the first weight from his wrapped weight and what I would end up with was an exact figure for an accessory-free Archie.

I could then keep a regular chart of his weight change and compare it with the information we'd received in our training notes. If the weight gain was a bit fast or a bit slow, I could modify his feeding a little to try to get it back on track. In fact Archie was pretty good; if anything a little slow to gain weight, but that might have been because he'd been orphaned so young and had to get used to unfamiliar food at such an early stage in his growth.

CHAPTER FIVE

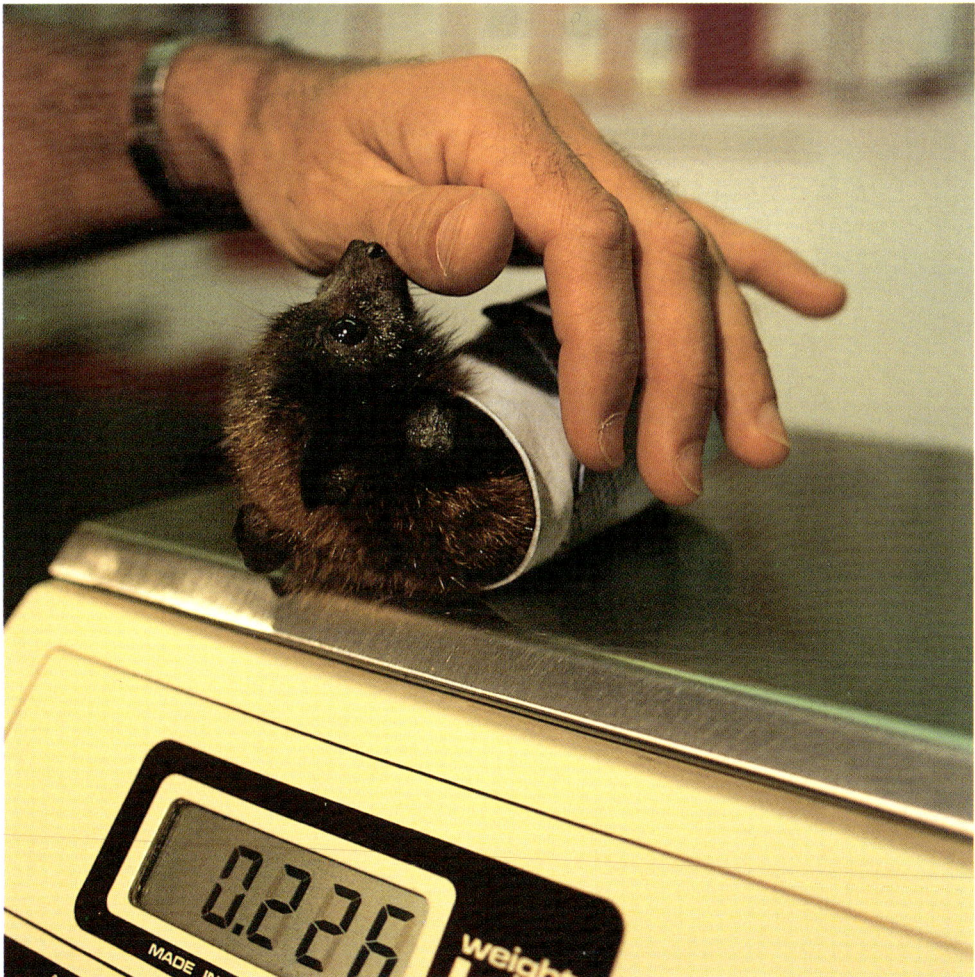

FOOD, GLORIOUS ... MESS

At about three weeks old Archie no longer needed to be kept warm inside my shirt because by then he could stabilise his own body temperature. He was still wrapped up in a handkerchief, but a bit more loosely, and quite often he'd wriggle out and do a bit of careful exploring in his cage. After feeding and grooming he'd often hang from my fingers and stretch out his wings before giving them a few strong flaps. This exercise was important to build up his muscles, because in a couple of months or so he'd be embarking on that most vital of adventures — flight.

I took him to work with me in his cage each day. It was an ideal way to transport him and provided a safe space for him to crawl around in if he wanted to.

SEASONED TRAVELLERS

When flying foxes leave their colony at dusk to search for food, they may travel long distances to get to a particular source of blossoms or fruit. Sometimes the journey may be as many as thirty or forty kilometres.

They are remarkably good navigators and seem to be able to memorise elements of the landscape below them so they can find their way back to the same spot time after time. Out in the bush they'll use reflections of moonlight on rivers or creeks to help guide them, but when they're close to cities they can use the lines of lights like a street map to keep them on course.

To navigate so well they need excellent eyesight. This is one of the ways in which flying foxes are different to the smaller bats. Many of those small bats rely on a sort of sonar system called echolocation to find their food and their way around. They make high-pitched squeaks and listen for the sound bouncing back from objects. To do that they've developed very sensitive ears and even specially shaped faces. Flying foxes don't have this ability.

Most of the small bats are insect eaters, but flying foxes are vegetarians. Once a flying fox finds its way to a particular tree, a good sense of smell helps it zero in on the food itself.

In later weeks I stuck a wooden crosspiece between the bars, and Archie would climb up and hang from it.

In my office I set up what came to be known as the 'Batmobile'. It was really a clothes-airer with some towelling or other material attached to it for Archie to grab on to securely while I worked at my desk.

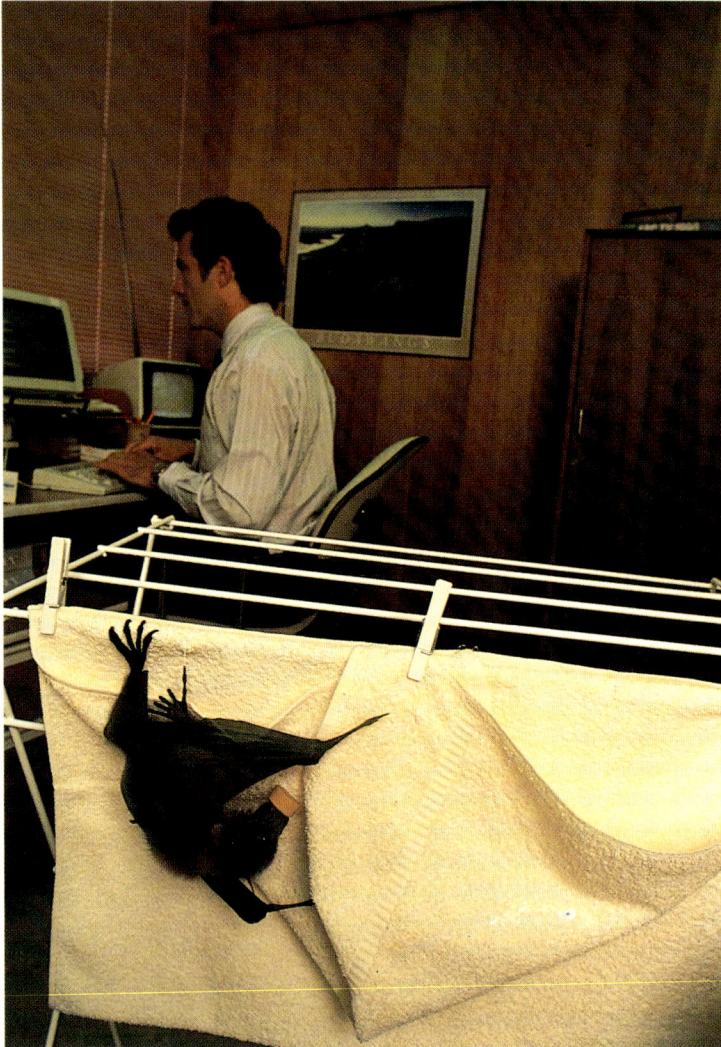

He'd hang there quite happily, occasionally flapping his wings, and watching people walk past the door.

There was still a lot of curiosity about this rather odd animal I was fostering and perhaps some uncertainty about the rather odd foster parent himself. After all, wandering round with a bat in your shirt or having a flying fox gymnasium in your office wasn't standard behaviour at the ABC. One of the senior journalists on 'The 7.30 Report' was renowned for his very funny impressions of other people on the staff and one afternoon as I wandered through the '7.30' office area I heard a group of people laughing loudly. When I found them, Geoff had just finished doing his comic routine, but one or two people insisted that he do his impression of me again now that I'd arrived.

'Of me?' I wondered. What strange eccentricities did I have? What embarrassing habits were about to be exposed? Without a word, and very solemnly, Geoff walked over to a nearby doorframe. Then, showing remarkable agility, he suddenly grabbed the top of it, hoisted himself up off the ground and hung upside-down, grinning, with his tie dangling next to his left ear. An extraordinary mix of flying fox and journalist!

Archie had grown well on the special milk formula he'd had for the first weeks of his fostering. At about two months old, though, he needed to start preparing to eat solid food. The first step was apple purée; you know, the sort you can buy in little jars or cans for human babies. Well, flying fox babies seem to like it too, or at least they do once they figure out how to eat it.

In the wild, babies would be introduced to fruit by licking the juice from around their mother's mouth when she returned from feeding, and even taking small pieces of chewed fruit from her. I didn't fancy smearing apple purée all around my lips, so my approach was a bit different.

Even so, introducing Archie to a spoonful of soft yellow mush was an interesting experience. He was meant to lap at it with his tongue. What he actually did was stick his face in it. Perhaps he was trying to suck it in like his milk, but that didn't work very well. So his nose came up out of the purée-filled spoon covered with creamy apple, and he sneezed, snuffled and shook his head around so that yellow goo spattered everywhere. (A large part of that everywhere was me.) Once he'd stopped sneezing he looked up. The fur all around his mouth and nose was covered in apple purée and the hairs were all stuck together, rather like a punk style on someone who had found some yellow hair gel. After that glance, which seemed to say, 'What was that I just put my face in?', he started to lick around his lips. After a few licks he decided his face was a good source of food and ignored the spoon.

Once he'd licked off as much as he could, I offered him the spoon again, but even flying foxes don't learn that fast. He plunged his head back into the mush, then sprayed it around just like before. I was glad I had a towel draped over me. He licked the apple from around his mouth and then dived back for another dose of purée.

It didn't take too many sessions before he'd figured out that it was better to lick directly from the spoon instead of feeding from his face. Not that that stopped him from spraying apple purée everywhere; as he no doubt reasoned, you should have fun when you feed.

The apple purée was introduced gradually into his diet. He still had his milk by itself, and sometimes he had a blend of the two. But the milk was being reduced and he was moving towards more solid food. After a week or so of purée, I tried him on some chopped steamed apple — soft, but not too mushy. He needed slowly to get used to the idea of fibre. Unlike us humans who (particularly these days) make an effort to get as much fibre into our diet as possible, flying foxes spit it out. Literally. When they're feeding in the wild on fruits or berries they chew them up in their mouth until all the juice has been sucked out and then spit out the leftover mess of skin and fibre. (This has led to the rather unpleasant folk-myth that flying foxes vomit while they're eating. But this isn't true at all!)

When Archie first came across fibre it was … well, it was a bit of a challenge. It didn't take him long to work out that chopped apple wasn't as good as purée if he only licked it. So he finally got a couple of small pieces into his mouth and made some cautious chewing motions. Then, as the juice squeezed out, he chewed with more

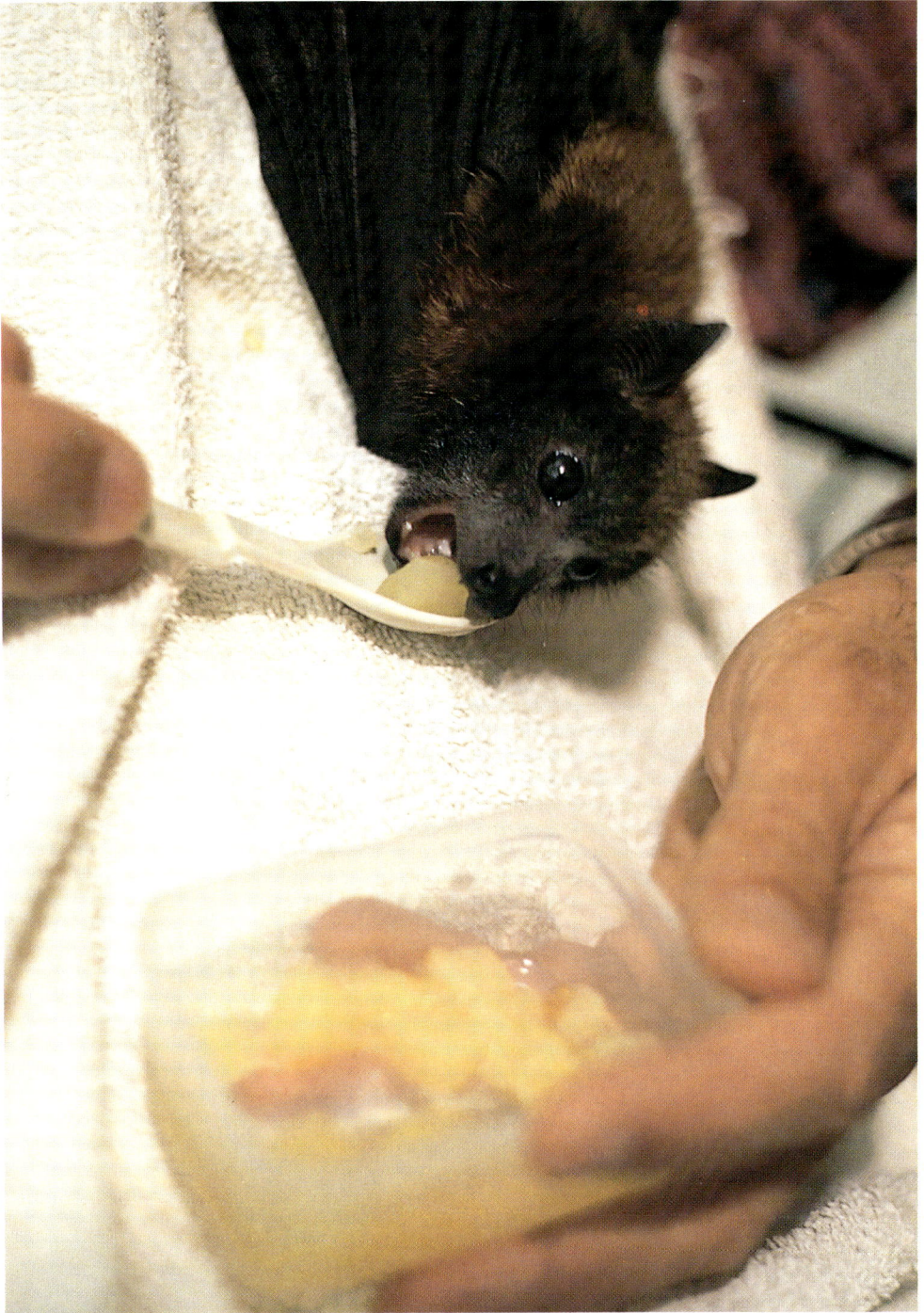

enjoyment. But after a while it was obvious that all the juice must have gone. He chewed a bit and then stopped. Chewed and stopped. He looked around. There was something in his mouth that he seemed to know he wasn't supposed to swallow, but he wasn't sure what else to do with it. He looked uncertain, like a child who has chomped excitedly on their first chewing-gum but isn't sure what to do when the flavour runs out.

There was more stop–start chewing on what must have been just a tasteless little ball of fibre before, either through instinct or good luck, it worked its way to the front of his mouth and dropped out. Then he was ready for more. He was confused by the resulting little fibre-ball again, but eventually it dropped out too.

It didn't take very long before Archie was spitting out fibre as if it was the most natural thing in the world. By ten or eleven weeks he was off the teat and eating apple mixed with his milk formula. Of course, with all this food going in, there was no shortage of material coming out at the other end. Obviously a flying fox can't wear nappies all its life, so for a while I'd been trying to toilet train Archie.

Imagine that you were hanging up somewhere from your toes. Suddenly you knew you had to go to the toilet. What would be your main concern — apart from wondering why you were there in the first place? Well, yes … to try to put it as delicately as possible, it would be that most of you was underneath the parts that were going to be producing the disagreeable substances, and you wouldn't want most of your body and head to become a rather messy target area. So what would you do? Well if you had to stay hanging on the branch, or whatever it was you were attached to, you might try to reach up, grab the branch with your hands, release your feet, and do what needed to be done while your head and body remained safely above the process.

And that is exactly what flying foxes do. It's called 'inverting'. While hanging from their feet, they reach up with their thumb claws, grab the branch, let go with their feet, go to the toilet, give themselves a quick shake and grab hold again with their feet. Quite gymnastic, but very effective; and certainly necessary when they have a digestive process whose normal healthy product we tend to think of as diarrhoea. So it was very important that Archie learned proper toilet skills.

Basically it meant getting him used to the idea of toileting while his head was higher than his feet. To begin with, that meant me holding him with his head up and gently rubbing his bottom or his genitals to get one or other of the processes going, with plenty of tissues on hand for when it worked. After a while, he would tend to hang onto my hand with his thumb claws for balance, and eventually I was delighted to see him hanging happily by his thumbs from the bar in his cage and relieving himself.

CHAPTER SIX

WE HAVE LIFT-OFF ...

As he grew, Archie became more mobile and more vocal. I can't remember quite how old he was when he first started making noises, but his trilling call became a frequent greeting. When I walked into the room, he'd call out from his cage. And sometimes he'd trill at me when he was hanging from the Batmobile in my office. It's hard to know exactly what the sound meant, but I usually responded by picking him up and giving him some attention, which he always seemed to like.

Orphaned flying foxes are very affectionate and like being handled. Archie always loved being tickled and massaged under his chin and round his chest and neck; if I stopped, he'd push his nose into my fingers to make me start again. He didn't like being touched on the back of the head, though. That's a general rule for flying foxes — they feel vulnerable there and don't appreciate being touched somewhere they can't see.

As I said, Archie also became a lot more mobile. By around ten weeks or so he'd become quite an agile climber and would heave himself around my T-shirt or up and down the legs of my jeans.

I also built him a sort of climbing frame of sticks, which he enjoyed exploring, and which gave him important exercise. It wouldn't be too long before he'd be clambering around in trees, and he needed to have the muscles to hang on with!

Once he got to the floor, though, he was clearly not in his element because he had to drag himself along on his stomach using his thumb-hooks. There's nothing much in the flying fox design to lift them off the ground for horizontal travel. Even so, if I called to him from the other side of the room, he'd scuttle across the carpet to me without too much trouble.

It became obvious as he got older what an alert and responsive animal he was. Over the weeks, a strong bond had been built up

between us. He knew me and my voice, would come when I called, and would single me out in a group of other people.

Flying foxes are being recognised by scientists as being quite intelligent, and there's even a suggestion that they've evolved from lemurs. Lemurs are the evolutionary step before monkeys, so, in a way, flying foxes could be related to us humans, because lemurs, monkeys, apes and humans are all part of the one group called primates. The brain of a flying fox is quite highly developed, so it's perhaps not too wild a speculation to suggest that flying foxes might be Australia's most intelligent native animals.

But however intelligent they are, there are some things they just don't figure out for themselves. And the most important one of all is flying. If a young flying fox hasn't learned to fly by four or five months old, then it probably never will. And that would mean it wouldn't survive in the wild. The whole point of fostering orphaned flying foxes like Archie isn't to make pets of them, but to give them the best possible chance of getting back into the wild where they belong. So making sure Archie could fly was one of the most important things I could do for him.

The funny thing is that for fostered flying foxes, flight doesn't seem to come naturally. They don't just go off for a quiet flap around by themselves even when they're old enough to do it. They need to be encouraged. I don't know how their mothers urge them to take the plunge under natural conditions, but as a foster-parent, you sometimes need to go to great lengths to get your baby airborne.

At about three months old they should begin their pilot training. There are various approaches but they all involve hanging your flying fox up somewhere in a room, moving back a short distance, and then calling to it. The idea is that to get across the room to you it will choose to fly.

When it was time for Archie's first lessons, I got out some step ladders, stuck a thick piece of wooden dowelling into one side, and wrapped a sock tightly around one end of the stick so Archie would have something reassuring to hang on to.

Of course you need to hang your flying fox high enough so that when it launches itself into the air, it's got enough height to give a couple of flaps without scraping its tummy after takeoff. So I hung Archie up about a metre or more above the ground, and backed away.

'Come on, Archie,' I called out. 'Come on ...' Archie hung and looked at me. He swayed a little on the piece of wood, shifting his weight from one foot to the other.

'Here. Here, Archie.' I patted my chest with my hands to show where I hoped the landing strip would be. Archie stretched out a thumb-claw towards me and made his high-pitched trilling call.

'No, I'm not coming to you. This time it's your turn to come to me. Come on. Over here.' I patted my chest again, feeling like a doubtful trainee Tarzan. Archie reached out again, swaying a bit more quickly. He obviously wanted to reach me, but he hadn't worked out how he could do it.

'Spread your wings, Archie. You need to flap. Spread them out.' How could I explain to him what he needed to do? How do you persuade a flying fox to flap its wings? Give encouragement? Set an example? Demonstrate perhaps? Well, why not …

Feeling very silly, I stuck my arms out and waved them up and down in what must have been one of the poorest imitations of flight since mediaeval adventurers glued on feathers and jumped off towers.

Certainly Archie didn't look impressed. If a flying fox can look puzzled, he looked puzzled.

'Archie, flap your wings. Flap!' I flapped. I made little squeaking noises with my tongue and teeth that I hoped sounded a bit like his trilling. My arms waved up and down and I added a few jumping motions which I hoped would encourage Archie to launch himself off the stick. I suspect I looked like a brolga which had failed its first dance class.

'Come on Archie, you're supposed to be learning to fly.' I stopped flapping and stood there with my hands on my hips. I don't know whether this was a better imitation of a flying fox spreading its wings, but suddenly Archie spread his. They stayed open for a couple of seconds and I thought, 'This is it!' But he slowly closed them again, shuffling awkwardly on the stick as if he was embarrassed at what he'd just done.

'I know it's the first time, but you have to learn this, Archie,' I said. 'Come on, flap your wings. Here, this is where you're aiming for.' I patted my chest again, and suddenly, without warning, his wings spread, his back arched, and he launched himself into the air.

The flight would only have taken a couple of seconds at the most, but I could see his face as he plunged towards me, his eyes bulging, effort, panic and surprise obvious in the stretched out neck and the frantic flaps. The small imaginary voice in my head was very clear. It said, 'WHAT AM I DOING??'

With a little thump he landed on my chest, his wings embracing me for an instant before he folded them and scrabbled up to my neck. He nuzzled in close to my jaw, looking for security after the terrifying trip into the unknown. I stroked him gently.

'Well done, Archie,' I said. 'Your first flight! Now you're really a *flying* flying fox.' He was still trembling under my fingers. I tried to imagine how confusing it must be, having only ever crawled around, to suddenly find yourself flapping in mid-air.

But mid-air needed to become familiar territory for Archie, so after a bit more stroking I put him back on his stick and started the whole process again. It didn't take quite as much persuasion to get him to make the leap off the stick the second time, but his approach to the landing strip was rather less accurate. To put it bluntly, I collected a faceful of flying fox; and that's no laughing matter when twelve claws are scrabbling to anchor themselves to your skin and scalp. I carefully detached Archie and went through some more practice flights, quite a few of which resulted in some very undignified landings — for both of us.

AGES AND STAGES

AGE IN WEEKS	IN THE WILD	FOSTERING
1-3	*Attached to mother's body. Hangs on to nipple even when not feeding. Temperature maintained through mother's body heat.*	*Wrapped firmly in hand-kerchief with nappy. Milk only, using teat and syringe. Dummy when not feeding. Extra warmth (heat pad or close to body) to regulate temperature.*
4	*Occasionally hangs on to branch by itself near mother. May support own weight on branch while suckling.*	*Starts to use Batmobile. Flaps wings often. Loose handkerchief wrapping. Can regulate own temperature.*
5	*Left hanging overnight in colony while mother goes out for food.*	*Sleeps hanging in cage with soft cloth nearby.*
8-9	*Licks juice from around mother's mouth and takes chewed food from her.*	*Starts on puréed fruit. Formula added to fruit, milk feeds reduced. No more dummy.*
10	*Starts to associate with other bats.* *Free from mother during daylight.*	*Tries chopped steamed apple. Actively climbing. Responds to calls.*
11	*Independence increases.*	*Feeds from own container. No more milk (all formula added to chopped fruit).*
12-13	*Takes short flights in colony.*	*Learns to fly at home. Leaves foster parent for creche cage with other orphans.*
14-15	*Socialising well in colony.*	*Socialising in creche.*

AGE IN WEEKS	IN THE WILD	FOSTERING
16	*Flies out with colony at night for food.*	*Transferred to release cage near colony.* *Wild flying foxes visit.* *All food supplied.*
20	*Integrated into life of colony.*	*Door of release cage opened. Accompanies wild flying foxes at night.* *Mix of natural and supplied food.* *Supplied food decreased.*
Anywhere between 24 and 35		*Does not return to cage.* *Integrated into colony.* *Door closed.*

(All figures are approximate. Individual flying foxes may vary significantly from these averages.)

After a few days, though, it was obvious that Archie had really come to enjoy our flying sessions (well, *his* flying sessions; I didn't need to flap any more), and had gained a lot of confidence. I'm pleased to say he'd also gained a lot of accuracy which made the whole process much more comfortable for me. So it looked as though the last big step in fostering Archie had been taken. There wasn't much more for me to do.

Archie was now just over three months old, and in only a few days it would be time for us to part company.

CHAPTER SEVEN

CAGES TO FREEDOM

As I mentioned at the beginning of this book, doing the WIRES training course for foster parents was an essential step before trying to look after a young flying fox. If I hadn't completed the course, there would have been so many things I wouldn't have done properly, and so many that would have been unexpected (and perhaps impossible) puzzles. As it was, most of the job of raising Archie went pretty much according to plan with no major crises. He didn't get any sort of lung infection, he had no major fungal problems, he fed well most of the time, he put on weight as he was supposed to, and he learned to fly relatively easily. What a model child!

Sometimes, though, it can be a real struggle for foster parents, and there can be times when with even the best care and attention, the little orphan dies. That's sad, of course, but it's important to remember that out in their natural environment quite a few babies die anyway through disease, losing their grip on their mother during flight, or seasonal food shortages.

Even though I didn't have any big problems with Archie, it was good to know there was a network of other people who were fostering flying foxes, some of whom were very experienced. They were always happy to offer advice or help (usually both) and were only a phone call away. Sometimes it was good to actually get together over a cup of coffee with other bat-minders to compare notes on how our little orphans were progressing. There were always stories to be shared and laughed over. Mind you, if we met in a cafe there were often very odd looks from other patrons as we sat with flying foxes hanging contentedly from our clothing.

Archie had been too big and too active for a while now to stay in his cage for any length of time, so he'd taken over the laundry (at my invitation). I'd expanded his climbing frame with some larger sticks and hung cloths from them so that he'd have the comforting sensation of soft material close to him. Almost like being in the midst

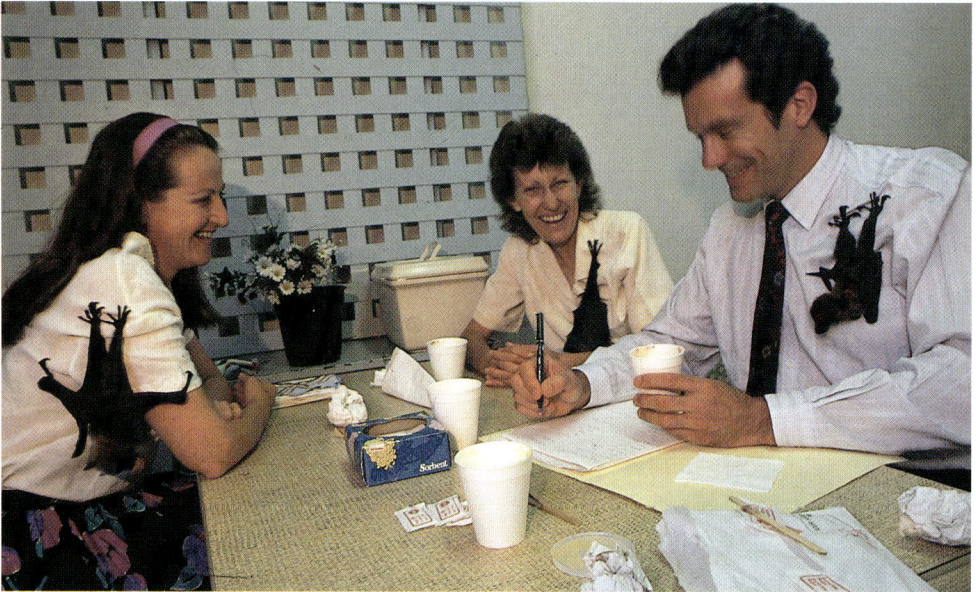

of a small colony! He used to clamber up and down with great skill and would launch himself off a branch, flapping through the air towards me, when I opened the door. The flying lessons had worked well! But he constantly wanted attention and it was obvious he needed a lot of company. It was also obvious that living with a human just wasn't quite enough somehow. Especially at night he'd become very active, chattering away, and I knew that out in the wild he would have been learning to get along with a whole family of other flying foxes. They're very social animals, so it's important that as they grow up they feel a part of a group. They can't just be bonded to one individual, and especially not if that individual happens to be a human being.

Although I wasn't looking forward to Archie leaving, I could feel that it was nearly time for him to go. His next challenge would be realising that he was a flying fox, not a human. Having been exclusively around people all the time since the first week of his life, he had no other sort of identity. Now he knew he could fly, he probably wondered why I didn't occasionally flap across the room and hang on the climbing frame with him, instead of it always being his turn to fly to me. After all, I was the same sort of creature that he was … wasn't I?

Establishing an identity as a flying fox amongst a group of other flying foxes was what the next stage of fostering was all about — except that before that happened the bond with the foster parent had to be broken. Archie had to learn to mix with his own kind and to recognise humans as different — perhaps even dangerous — forms of life. That change had to happen slowly and carefully, but it wasn't a process I could be a part of. That's why, now that Archie could take to the air, we had to say goodbye.

All the flying foxes that had been fostered by people like myself had to be handed in at around three months old, provided they'd reached a weight of at least 300 grams. That was a size where they were considered sturdy enough to begin the adaptation to life in the wild. Officials from WIRES and the Ku-ring-gai Bat Colony Committee made sure that each young flying fox was weighed and had its forearm bones measured to keep a record of its growth. Detailed records were also taken of where they had been found, how old they were and what health problems they may have had. Then a metal band was attached to one of the thumb-claws, so that if at some time in the future an individual was found dead, it could be identified, and the location of its body, its age and apparent cause of death used to help with research information on flying foxes.

As the metal band fastened around Archie's thumb, squeezed into place by special pliers, I found myself hoping that no-one would have to read the information on that little ring — not for many years to come anyway. I knew Archie was going to have to face the many risks of the natural environment — not to mention the hazards of living in a colony close to the city — but I wanted him to be safe, and I wanted him to enjoy his freedom.

That band on Archie's thumb was the signal that our time together had ended. From that point on, he could no longer be my responsibility, and I had to hand him over. For myself, and for everybody else who'd fostered a little orphan, having to say that final goodbye wasn't easy.

But while there was sadness at having to part, there was a great sense of achievement, too. As foster parents we'd succeeded in what was sometimes a difficult job. We'd given our young flying foxes the chance of a new life; a natural, wild life. And that was something to feel good about.

I wasn't part of the next stage in Archie's return journey to the wild. I was just told about it later. But this is what happened ...

After measuring and banding the young flying foxes, it was party time! (For them, not the foster parents.) All the youngsters went into a big aviary together so they could start to socialise. It must have been like a mass blind date, since many of them had never even seen another flying fox before, let alone had the chance to sniff one, chatter

at one and have it chatter back, or just hang around in a group together.

In this large cage there were also some adult flying foxes who had been rescued and were recovering from injuries, or who couldn't be released because some problem they had (like an inability to fly) meant that they wouldn't survive in the wild. These adults were useful in the cage because they started to teach the young orphans about social structure and how to behave in a colony. The youngsters had to learn, for example, that the most senior bats took the best and highest hanging positions; being in the wrong place at the wrong time would earn a young flying fox a sharp prod from a grown-up's thumb-claw. They were also learning to feed in a group and, most importantly of all, to feel part of a group. Of course, they were still dependent on humans for their daily food and drink, but it was a big step towards a life in the wild.

The next step, however, was the final one. After spending three or four weeks in the nursery or creche cage, all the fostered orphans were transferred to another large cage very close to the flying fox colony. This was the only colony left in the Sydney area, so almost certainly all of the orphans would have been born in that same colony four or five months before.

The release cage, as it was called, was in a secret location. Only a small number of people knew where it was, and there was a simple reason for that; the less contact the orphan group had with humans, the better. No casual visitors, no pining foster parents wanting another last goodbye, no curious photographers or researchers. Food was delivered quickly and quietly so that each day the young flying foxes forgot more and more about their contact with humans. And each night their identity as flying foxes would be strengthened. The wild ones would visit ...

It didn't take long after the orphans were put into the release cage for the wild flying foxes to find them. The colony wasn't far away, and as the wild ones flew out at dusk, they were often drawn to the release cage by the calls of the youngsters. Hanging on the outside of the cage the wild flying foxes would sniff at them, becoming familiar with their scent and the sound of their chattering. For the orphans, it was their first chance to meet some of the members of the colony they would soon become part of.

Another few weeks later, it was time for the last step in this final stage. As the food was delivered by whoever was looking after the cage, the door was deliberately left wide open. That night when the wild flying foxes came to visit, they would be able to enter the cage, and the orphans, if they wanted to, would be able to leave it.

The idea was that the young flying foxes would decide to head off on what would be, for them, an extraordinary adventure. As the wild ones visited and then flew out to search for food, the orphans could go with them. If they then wanted to come back to the safety and familiarity of the cage at the end of the night, they could. Or, if they chose to fly on with their newly found wild family back to the colony, they could do that instead. Over the following days and nights that the cage door was left open, the orphans that chose to return found that their human-delivered food supply got smaller. Not that they were starved of food. It was simply that as their food intake from the wild increased, they didn't eat as much in the cage. So the next day they were given a bit less. That way, as the orphans chose more and more to find natural food with the colony members, they became less and less dependent on feeding in the cage.

It didn't take long before all the orphans were flying out at night. But many of them kept coming back to the cage, either to hang in it during the day, or simply to hang near it in one of the surrounding trees. It was important to let the young flying foxes become a part of the colony gradually, so there was no sense of pressuring them to leave the area. As time passed, more and more of them chose to spend both days and nights with their wild family, but it was a slow process. There were still some who needed the continuing familiarity of the cage and a small amount of supplied food. Their numbers were dwindling, though, and eventually there were only two or three stragglers left. Finally, after almost 50 nights, none of the orphans came back to the cage. That morning, the door was closed.

Archie was back where he really belonged, and it was good to know that it had all gone well. But for me, there was a strong, last memory from weeks before. Just after Archie had had the band put on his thumb-claw, I held him up in front of me. Of course, he didn't know what was going to happen next, and as he hung, quite relaxed, from my fingers, he looked around. His ears twitched back and forth just as they had on the first morning we met, and his eyes were alert and sparkling with curiosity as unfamiliar people moved around near him. I stroked him under his chin and on the soft fur at the top of his chest. He was so warm, so full of life. I remember holding this little animal that had so much promise for the future, and thinking, 'This is what it was all for, Archie, all that caring and looking after you. Now you're ready for your *real* life to start.'

Then I held him close to my face and brushed my nose against his fur, breathing in his familiar scent one last time. Perhaps he realised then that something important was about to happen, because he moved away from my face and hung quite still for a moment. I looked at him. He looked at me. I handed him over.

Before I met Archie, I'd have laughed at anyone who told me that one day I'd miss the feeling of a flying fox's thumb-claw up my left nostril. But I do. And the dirty nappies. And the struggles under the bathroom tap. Spending a few months of my life with such an intelligent and entertaining animal was a rich and rewarding experience. Now, as I see occasional flying foxes in the night sky near the city, I often wonder if one of them is Archie. Wherever he is, I hope he flies safely through many nights to a long and healthy life in the wild.

A FEW LAST WORDS

After reading this book you may be thinking, 'I'd like to do the same thing and look after an orphaned native animal'. Well, that might be possible, but it's important to remember that you must have proper training (otherwise you could do more harm than good) and that there are strict laws about keeping native animals or birds even for short periods of time.

If you're interested in helping native wildlife, then the best idea is to contact a conservation group in your area and ask their advice about what you can do. There are various groups in different states, (WIRES, for example, is not a national organisation) but through some of the larger bodies like the World-Wide Fund for Nature (WWF), the Australian Conservation Foundation (ACF), Greenpeace and the Wilderness Society, you should be able to find some way of making a really practical contribution to protecting and preserving our wildlife.

While I was writing this book and making the film which came before it, a few people asked me why I was devoting all this time and effort to a flying fox, which is not usually a very popular animal. Well, that lack of popularity is actually part of the answer. I believe we need to appreciate even the traditionally disliked animals (like bats, snakes, spiders and so on), and start to understand that they all have an important role to play. They deserve our respect and concern, too, even if they're not quite as appealing as koalas, baby seals or dolphins.

The important thing is to make the move from liking individual animals to appreciating the big picture. When I was a child, I used to go looking for lizards, frogs and all sorts of insects amongst the rocks and logs in the fields near our house. But as I've got older, the exciting thing has been learning about the connections between all those individual creatures. Everything depends on everything else. The connections may vary but one way or another, every type of animal and plant in a particular environment is somehow linked.

That means that every form of life is important because it has its own place in the wild. Each one depends on certain other animals and plants, and a lot of other ones depend on it. The end result is like a huge jigsaw puzzle where all the pieces fit together and when the puzzle's complete everything works beautifully.

What we humans have managed to do is make a huge mess of this wonderful jigsaw. There are still a lot of pieces sticking together, but there are a lot that we've either broken or lost completely. We've chopped down the forests, we've polluted the air and water, and we've hunted many animals and birds into extinction. For hundreds of years, we've shown a complete lack of respect for the environment. To put it bluntly, we've killed off big chunks of our world.

One way to start repairing the damage is to understand how those jigsaw pieces fit together. And that brings us back to Archie and the example of the flying fox. Certainly flying foxes can be a problem for fruitgrowers, but why have they become a pest? It's because we've cleared away most of their natural food-trees, so they have to find something else to eat. We've taken a piece out of the jigsaw by removing those trees, and we've disturbed the natural balance. In killing off hundreds of thousands of flying foxes over the years we've also failed to recognise the important part that flying foxes play in the jigsaw. They help to distribute the seeds and pollen of the native trees they feed in, and that means they help new trees to grow. Flying foxes give the forests new life.

So that's an important part of why I wrote this book. What I'm hoping is that if you enjoyed meeting Archie, you might think more about flying foxes and their role in the environment, and from there perhaps you might think further and ask yourself about how other animals, birds, insects, reptiles, fishes, trees and flowers fit into their places in that enormous puzzle. Finding the answers will take you on some wonderful voyages of discovery, through books and films and photographs, and perhaps better still, out into the wild itself. And as you start to realise that it does all fit together, you'll also understand that the wild needs protection and care; in a different way perhaps, but just as much as a defenceless little orphan.

We've done a lot of damage to our world in the past and we're still hurting it today. If, as you've read this book, you've come to care about Archie, then I'd ask you to put some of that caring back into the wild world he's now a part of.

ACKNOWLEDGEMENTS

Warmest thanks to:

Dione Gilmour and Richard Campbell of the ABC's Natural History Unit, for initiating, supporting and producing the film *Raising Archie*.

Helen George, for sharing a wealth of experience in flying fox foster-parenting, and especially for her instruction manuals and growth charts.

Paul Sweeney and Michael Rayner, for wonderful photographs that tell the story better than any words.

Linda Collins, Heather Parsons and Julie Spence, for invaluable assistance and advice, as well as participation in some of the photographs.

Don Henry, Director of WWF Australia, for essential advice and encouragement.

Harry Wever, for veterinary guidance.

Sue Sellers, for being Archie's rescuer and ever-helpful babysitter.

George Szilasi, for setting me off on the right track.

Brigit Brunken, for assistance and foster-parenting advice.

Sharne Weidland, for an important chapter in Archie's life.

Kerryn Parry-Jones, for research information.

All the staff of WIRES, especially Mikla Lewis.

Nancy Pallin and the Ku-ring-gai Bat Colony Committee, for information, and for their support for and protection of Sydney's flying foxes.

Kirsty Melville of Simon & Schuster for asking me to write this book and encouraging me through the process.

Susan Morris-Yates of Simon & Schuster, for patience, flexibility and perception in the editing process.

And especially Catherine, who shared many of the experiences of raising Archie with me.

PICTURE CREDITS

Michael Rayner pages 6, 8, 10, 12, 14, 16, 17, 18 (both), 19 (both), 20 (both), 22, 23, 24, 26, 27 (both), 28, 29 (both), 30, 48, 50, 70

Paul Sweeney pages 2, 3, 5, 12, 39, 45, 46, 53, 57, 59 (both), 60, 61, 62, 63, 64, 65, 68, 72, 73, 74, 77

Bill Bachman/ANT Photo Library page 32
G. B. Baker/ANT Photo Library page 49 (left)
Pavel German/ANT Photo Library page 49 (right)
Ken Griffiths/ANT Photo Library pages 36 and 67